TREVOR WYE

Flute Secrets

Advice for students,
teachers and professionals

Second Edition

T0039832

With contributions by Susan J. Maclagan

A notebook of professional matters which deals with the purchase, performing, teaching and the repair and alteration of flutes.

Written by Trevor Wye
Editor and advisor: Susan J. Maclagan

TREVOR WYE

Flute Secrets

Advice for students, teachers and professionals

Second Edition

Every effort has been made to trace the copyright holders
of the photographs in this book but one or two were unreachable.
We would be grateful if the photographers concerned would contact us.

Illustrations by Joanna Hegemann.

ISBN: 978-1-78558-603-3

Novello

EXCLUSIVELY DISTRIBUTED BY
HAL•LEONARD®

Visit Hal Leonard Online at
www.halleonard.com

Contact Us:
Hal Leonard
7777 West Bluemound Road
Milwaukee, WI 53213
Email: info@halleonard.com

In Europe contact:
Hal Leonard Europe Limited
Distribution Centre, Newmarket Road
Bury St Edmunds, Suffolk, IP33 3YB
Email: info@halleonardeurope.com

In Australia contact:
Hal Leonard Australia Pty. Ltd.
4 Lentara Court
Cheltenham, Victoria, 3192 Australia
Email: info@halleonard.com.au

FOREWORD

For over 60 years, Trevor Wye has gathered 'secrets' about the flute, stemming from his studies with Geoffrey Gilbert and Marcel Moyse, and growing through his experiences as a freelance performer and now as one of the most notable flute educators in the world. Perhaps his best-known published works are the *Practice Books for the Flute* and *Marcel Moyse, an Extraordinary Man: A Musical Biography*. There is no doubt that Trevor commands one of the best understandings of flute customisation, technique and development in the modern age. When the initial manuscript for 'Flute Secrets' arrived, we knew this was going to be something special.

A constant message throughout this book is that every flute and every player is unique. It takes time to find the right combination, and trial and error to discover which 'quick fixes' and customisations work best for you. Trevor has compiled his findings in this book, ranging from simple fixes — such as preventing leaking keys — to resourceful 'hacks' — such as adding filler to tone holes and making your own 'sound bridges' to improve resonance! Further to flute specifics, you'll also find essential advice on developing your career as a performing musician or teacher, including etiquette, music copyright and practice strategies. Every experienced player will wish they had this earlier in life, but better late than never!

Trevor shares his fascinating experiences as an educator and performer who has travelled the world, and his enthusiasm for all flute matters is infectious, which makes for an entertaining and informative read. He collaborates here with freelance flutist, teacher and author of *A Dictionary for the Modern Flutist*, Susan J. Maclagan.

This is an invaluable resource for flutists, tutors, students and musicians alike. Although we would recommend you explore the book by dipping in and out, you can read page by page if you prefer. Use the contents pages to find a topic of your choosing, and then delve into the wisdom that this book holds. We hope you discover secrets you may never have come across before.

Sam Lung and Louise Unsworth
The Editors
Novello & Co

Table of Contents

1.4 **Head joint and flute variables**

1.5 **Customising your flute**

1.6 **The piccolo**

1.7 **Transporting flutes**

SECTION 2 EDUCATIONAL ASSISTANCE

2.1 **Practising**

2.2 Practice schedules

2.3 Tone

2.4 Technical practice

2.5 Articulation practice

2.6 A guide to faster progress

2.7 **Flute literature**

2.8 **Special and sensitive fingerings**

2.9 **Trills**

SECTION 3 PROFESSIONAL STRATEGIES

3.1 **Performing**

3.2 **Helping your career**

3.3 **Competitions**

3.4 **Performance practice — an introduction**

3.5 **Performance practice — Baroque music**

3.6 **Performance practice — Classical music**

3.7 **Nineteenth-century bravura**

3.8 **Contemporary music**

3.9 **Career strategies**

3.10 Copyright and photocopying

3.11 Health issues

SECTION 4 TEACHING STRATEGIES

4.1 Teaching strategies

4.2 Setting up a teaching space

4.3 Practice plans

4.4 Student performing problems

4.5 Fun stuff

SECTION 5
EAR TRAINING, PLAYING IN TUNE, FLUTE TUNING AND REPAIRS

5.1 Ear training, playing in tune, flute tuning and repairs

5.2 Dealing with other problem notes

5.3 **Test your tuning skills**

5.4 **Repairs and adjustments**

5.5 **Some experiments to try**

Bibliography

PREFACE

There will be much in this book which is hardly secret to the experienced orchestral player, and much of it will be seen as 'old hat'! Yet to some players there will be information which I hope will prove useful, especially to younger players starting out on their careers. Teachers too may find some interesting facts which may help them to help others.

There are some technical details which a number of players may find tricky to understand, though I have tried hard to make these accessible, especially to those who have an aversion to maths.

The advice offered does not attempt to replace a knowledgeable teacher but might supplement or reinforce what they have to say.

Trevor Wye
2017

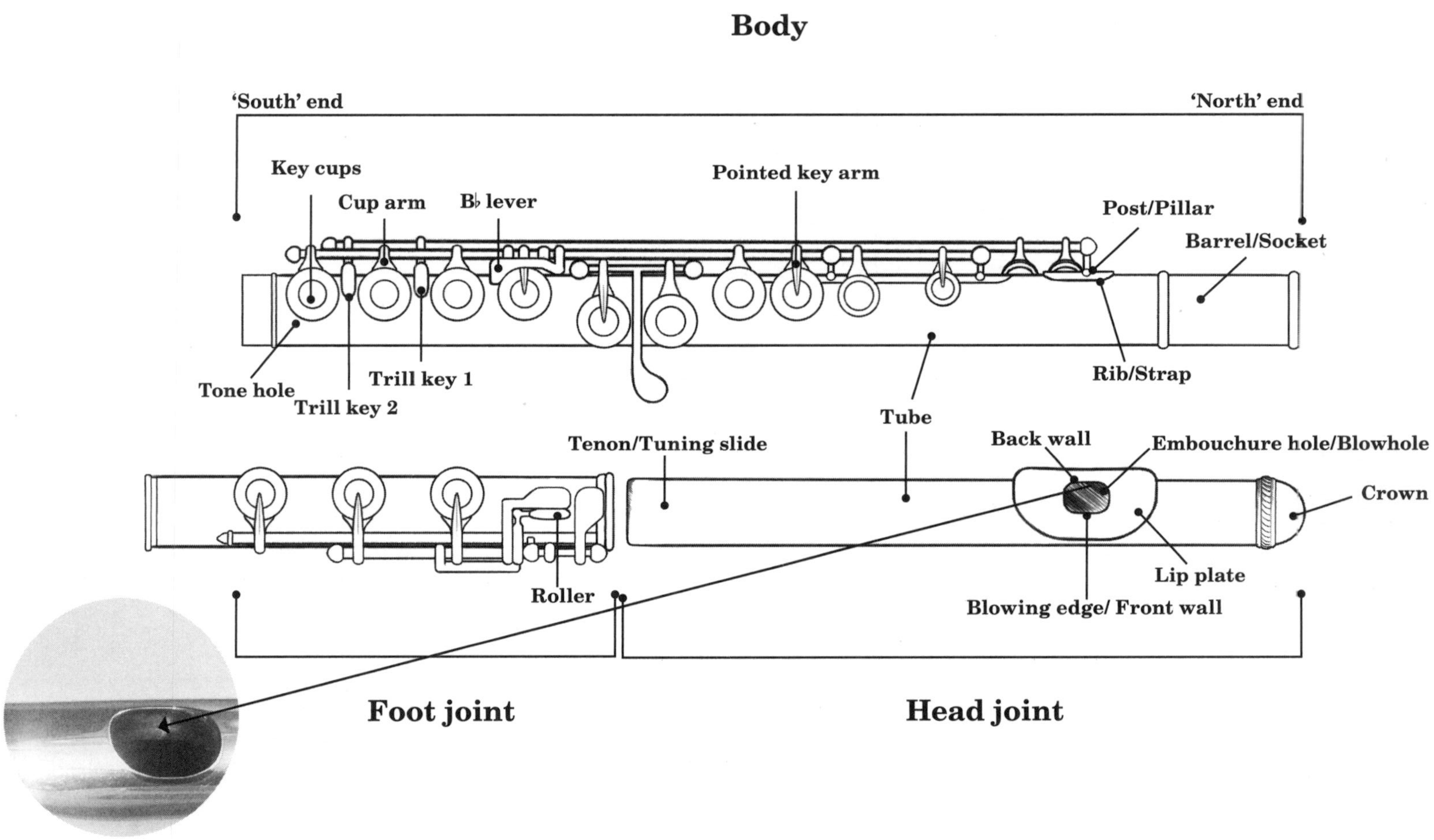

Body

'South' end   'North' end

Key cups

Cup arm   B♭ lever

Trill key 1

Trill key 2

Tone hole

Pointed key arm

Post/Pillar

Barrel/Socket

Rib/Strap

Tube

Tenon/Tuning slide

Roller

Embouchure hole/Blowhole

Crown

Back wall

Lip plate

Blowing edge/ Front wall

Head joint

Foot joint

Names of Notes

The lowest note on our flutes is either B or C— known as B_1 or C_1. An octave higher is B_2 or C_2, and so on. This is how we refer to notes throughout the book.

The left-hand trill key (next to the right-hand first finger) is known as T_1, and the right-hand trill key is known as T_2.

Looking at the flute from above, with the head joint to the left, the right-hand end is referred to as 'south' and the left-hand end as 'north'.

Names of Mechanism Keys

These are the names of the mechanism keys used throughout this book.

It is appreciated that players might, for example, refer to the right-hand third-finger key as the 'D' key, but as you can see below, it is this tone hole which emits 'E' and the key covering it, more logically, is called the 'E' key.

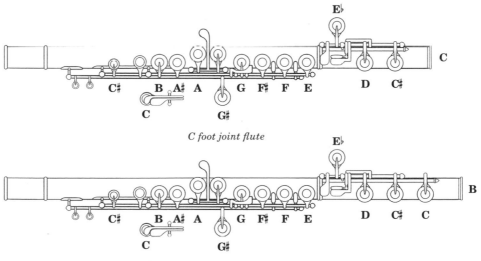

C foot joint flute

B foot joint flute

1

Section 1

The Instrument

1.1 FLUTE PURCHASE

OVERVIEW

If you take advice from a respected player, it is worth checking if they are a supporter of a particular brand — likewise when taking advice from sales assistants. In some cases, the flute manufacturer will be reputable, but in other cases the companies may have sponsored or compensated them for their loyalty. This isn't to say that the advice offered is worthless, but just take care.

The choice of flutes is bewildering. Even flutes from the same manufacturer can have dissimilar characteristics; the head joints can be different from each other, incorporating a variety of lip plates and risers, not to mention the tube shape, cut of the embouchure hole, and even the position of the lip plate on the head joint. There is also no consensus on the flute scale between manufacturers, that is, the size and placement of the tone holes which give the flute its pitches. Each flute is entirely unique.

Not everyone is familiar with facts and figures about flute construction, but it's useful to understand how differing factors can affect the response, playability and the subsequent purchase of a fine and reliable flute.

THE CHOICE

When buying a flute, choose the head joint and the body separately. If they are by the same manufacturer, they are commonly made in different parts of the factory and only the fitting of the head joint to the body can be termed 'matched'. This may seem strange, but this is also quite usual for other instruments such as the violin, clarinet, bassoon and brass instruments — the bow, mouthpiece or crook are often purchased separately. Most professional flute players will use a different head joint on their favourite flute.

Find a specialist flute shop or visit the trade stands at a flute convention to give yourself the widest choice. Test new head joints by comparing them against your usual head joint — or ask for advice. Almost all flute manufacturers distribute the flute as a whole, but now shops increasingly allow a different head joint to be purchased with the chosen flute, regardless of brand. This is the way to go, and the end result will prove to be a more satisfactory purchase.

WOODEN FLUTES

Wooden flutes are now quite widely available, with some players suggesting that they blend better with the other woodwinds. This sounds logical, though the consideration of material is likely less significant than how the flute is played and, in particular, the tone quality used. That said, some materials and flutes 'invite' the player to formulate a particular kind of tone. Period orchestras and even some symphony orchestras prefer players to use wooden instruments for those compositions written before the middle of the 19th Century, and some even after this time. The most common wood used is known as African Blackwood or, more correctly, *Mpingo* or *Grenadilla* wood, both which are grown in Africa. It is dense, heavy and hard, making it ideal for musical instruments as it resists moisture.

1.2 HEAD JOINTS

HEAD JOINTS IN GENERAL

When playing, we listen to ourselves from only a few inches away — the distance between our ears and the flute. To appreciate what the audience is experiencing, either record your tone on a high-quality recording device. If you are not sure, always ask someone to listen.

Over the past 50 years at conventions and festivals, I have seen many new head joint devices claiming to improve the tone, response, intonation, pitch control and just about anything else you care to name. There are several different designs of cork replacements and stoppers. The buyers of these innovations usually (but not always) discard them in time, but the main goal has already been achieved: you have parted with your money. See also Section 5.5, *Crowns*.

Providing that the cork is placed in the correct position and it doesn't leak, all should be well. To check for leakage, place your hand over the open end of the head and blow hard into it with your lips covering the embouchure hole. There should be total resistance. According to some websites and repairpeople, the cork should be regularly replaced. Not necessarily. Provided it has been properly fitted, it should last many years. Some cork assemblies do seem more prone to leakage, perhaps due to design, and so it is better to check them yourself from time to time. You will find more information on corks in Section 5.4, *The head joint and cork*.

From time to time, attachments are seen which claim to radically improve your playing or the response of the flute. Attachments between the head, the body and, more commonly, attachments to the foot joint have appeared and may be used by prominent performers for a month or so before becoming history. The only noticeable change to the player seems to be a lightness of purse, though some of these gadgets might make a small difference. As new ones appear, try them out, but ask yourself before parting with your cash: does it make an *advantageous* difference or would you be better off practising?

CHOOSING A HEAD JOINT

First, choose two or three head joints which seem to be likely candidates, checking the overall response of each and how it feels and plays in general. Find ways of obtaining a good sound over all three octaves. First, play in the low register and check for fullness and quality of tone. Then, use the tune below to see if the same tone can be carried from the lower part of the second octave through to the upper part of the middle register without it becoming thin. Some head joints will not allow this.

Bear in mind that a head joint's character needs to be discovered and it might take some time to uncover this.

Tone Exercise: Into the middle register
Fig. 1.1

Finally, play the same melody an octave higher to check the third octave for fullness and quality.

Some flutes and head joints respond well in the first two octaves, but on rising to the third octave, the tone becomes noticeably thinner. It is easy to make a head joint play the low notes well, a little more difficult with the second octave, and less common to find one which keeps the fullness of tone with plenty of harmonics into the upper octave. Play any favourite melody that ascends into the third octave several times to get accustomed to listening for any thinness when ascending — slow scales will also serve this purpose well. Often, a player will try several head joints, but will come back to the one which initially gave the best response.

Whilst there may be many head joint styles from which to choose, the embouchure hole is fairly uniform. For example, there may be attachments such as wings (see Fig. 1.4) or even odd-shaped lip plates. Try them, but be wary of these oddities; some head joints are appealing at first, but after time the novelty may wear thin and its purchase regretted.

The reader might wonder why it isn't possible to make all head joints the same. In engineering, which is essentially what flute manufacturing is, it isn't possible to make an *exact* copy of an object. It can be made within certain limits, but not *exactly*. There are so many small variables in head joint manufacture which affect the instrument's response; a flute maker can only try to make a head joint as close as possible to an excellent model.

To test a head joint for the overall compass (the whole range of the instrument), play the Fauré *Sicilienne* and transpose it up one semitone at a time, until you have tested about 6 or 7 keys. Another good tune to try is Gaubert's *Madrigal*. In the Gaubert, play the first 4 bars, then repeat it an octave higher. In the Fauré, check the tone quality when rising to B♭2, and in the Gaubert when rising to G2. If possible, play them both a semitone higher, followed by a tone higher. As before, listen for any thinness of tone in the third octave.

These are just a couple of examples, because they contain easy arpeggios and scales making it easy to both hear and check. Intonation problems are easier to hear in arpeggios than scales.

Fauré: Sicilienne
Fig. 1.2

Gaubert: Madrigal
Fig. 1.3

WINGS

Some lip plates have 'wings' of various shapes and sizes. These raised wing-shaped attachments to either side of the embouchure hole — one example shown below — were first suggested by Maximilian Schwedler in the 19th Century and were more commonly known as the 'Reform' lip plate.

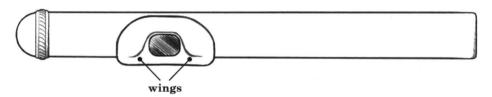

The 'Reform' lip plate
Fig. 1.4

Doublers and jazz players seem to like them because the wings help to direct the air more easily and as a result the players can pick up their flutes after playing the sax or clarinet and play reasonably well, without any embouchure fuss. Other players feel that with 'wings', they have less control and fewer tone colour changes. Each player must decide what is best for them. To check their effect with a regular head joint, see Section 5.5, *Adding wings.* You may have observed that most professional players perform on a standard-shaped head without wings.

THE LIP PLATE

These are offered in a variety of precious metals and the difference has more to do with cost than the resultant sound, though it should be pointed out that in a flute factory, the better and more experienced craftsmen are assigned to working with more expensive materials. Many players believe that lip plate materials make much less tonal difference than the 'chimney' (riser) of the lip plate. Having tried many hundreds of head joints, I feel that the tube shape, the exact placement of the lip plate on the tube and, even more importantly, the cut of the embouchure hole, has a greater effect on tone than the material of which it is made.

The shape of the lip plate has been the subject of experimentation for many years. In the past 20 years or so, the part of the lip plate that you blow against — the 'front wall' — has been angled to create a sharper top edge. This is said to improve the response in the third octave. On some flutes, the rear section which is against the lip has also been bent towards the tube and reshaped to accommodate the preferences and jaw shapes of different players. This means that for most players, they have to turn the head joint inwards to get the blowing wall at the correct angle. Unless that is what you want, it may lead to disappointment in the long term — turning the head joint in too far may result in a flat-pitched and buzzy tone, or put another way, it may result in flat harmonics.

THE RISER

The hole in the lip plate where we blow into is commonly called the 'blowhole', or 'riser'. The variations in response, where different risers are made of different metals, has more to do with the fact that each one is *different*. A lip plate, riser, flute tube, flute, or indeed any metal object such as a door key, cannot be copied *exactly* as was outlined above. An engineer will confirm this and stipulate that an object may only be copied *within certain limits*. So, two flutes, two head joints, two lip plates and two risers will all be a little different from each other, even when made by the same person, using the same tools and materials and — as far as is possible — with *the same measurements*.

The big flute manufacturers currently offer a mixture of materials and although the tube may be of silver or gold, the lip plate and risers may be of other precious metals. Try them all. It is foolish to assume that a head with a gold or platinum riser will be better than a silver one. The laws of acoustics are not governed by the market price of precious metals. Don't be *gold struck.*

After initially testing several head joints, narrow down the field quickly. If you choose from too many at a session, it can lead to confusion and difficulty remembering which one does what. For some reason, the first choice often ends up as the best choice. It is better to give a longer trial to the final two or three.

Finally, check the octaves from G_1 to G_2, rising chromatically in octaves, then C_2 to C_3. Occasionally, a good head joint may also play flat octaves, the upper note being flatter than it should be. If the octaves are wrong, it may be that the maker placed the lip plate a fraction too far towards the flute body on a slightly wider part of the head joint.

For those who can afford it, and for a lifetime strategy, it is better to have two good head joints; the second-best one can always be available for sale if it can be replaced by one better than the first!

A good head joint may improve the tone and response of a flute, but it won't correct a poorly-made instrument or a faulty scale.

THE BLOWING EDGE — THE 'CARROT GRATER'

On some head joints, the blowing edge may have been sharpened to the point of being almost dangerous. The design is known colloquially as a 'carrot grater' and may well give the impression that the tone is rich and full of harmonics, and the articulation clear and instantaneous. The 'carrot grater' can encourage you to play with strong harmonics and sound almost oboe-like. If this is your wish, fine, but in the long run you may be dissatisfied by your purchase. It is easy to think that a given head joint is a great improvement just because it sounds different. The effect of the 'carrot grater' is also to make you believe your articulation is clearer. Only practice will do that.

There are repairpeople who will blunt an over-sharp blowing edge on request. This process is easily done. It simply involves taking away the sharp edge by gentle burnishing. This can be reversed if required and is not a difficult procedure.

1.3 FLUTES

CHOOSING A FLUTE

For the lower and middle registers, check for tone quality, ease, comfort and response. Most players begin by checking the lower end of the scale for the strength of the lowest notes, but when doing this, be sure that the tone does not become thinner or lacking in roundness at any point as you descend. It can easily be detected: play with a full tone and if at some point when descending (perhaps at a particular note) the tone narrows and lacks a roundness and sufficient fundamental, go back a note or two and play those few notes again to be sure. Of course, this narrowing of tone may be how you normally play, but you may already know that. You may recognise it as rather buzzy, perhaps with strong harmonics. You just need to be sure that the flute has an even tone down to its lowest notes.

Now, move from the lower octave to the second octave using the 'Aus Liebe' tune from Bach's *Passion According to St Matthew* (Fig. 1.5). Play the first note, A, with one tone colour and *keep that colour into the second octave.* After trying the passage a couple of times, change to another colour and repeat. If the E2 cracks easily when using a rich tone colour, try another flute or head joint because it might just be you. A reliable test is to use a hard and rich tone with plenty of harmonics for A1, and to then maintain that tone when ascending to E2. It will help you make a decision because some heads and flutes will not allow middle E to be played with a rich and dark tone, and will split or crack if pushed too hard. If the head joint will not allow you to keep the same colour, you may be forced into raising the air stream to prevent the note from cracking. If this happens, you may be playing with two entirely different tone colours for each octave — not a very wise move. What causes the middle notes to crack could be any number of technical or constructional reasons, or to do with the dimensions and shape of the blow hole, but it is not a flute and head joint combination that you need.

What follows are simple tuning checks which are set out in more detail in Section 5.1, *Check the tuning of your flute,* but for now the following simple checks will give you an idea about the flute's intonation.

Try the middle register tone with Bizet's 'Entr'acte' from *Carmen* (Fig 1.6), both *piano* and *forte*. To begin, first overblow middle E♭ to its next harmonic, B♭2 above, and compare the harmonic B♭2 with the natural B♭2. It should be *almost* exactly the same pitch as the natural note. Then check the B♭2 and C3 in the fourth bar and the D3 in the fifth bar for pitch. The D3 is often flat which may be due to the G tone hole being placed too low. When D3 is followed by E♭3, normally a very sharp note, the D3 can sound even flatter than usual. In this melody, the sequence B♭2, C3, D3 and E♭3 may not be perfectly in tune, but should be easily manageable on a good scale flute.

Repeat what you did with the 'Entr'acte', in a new key: E major. The first note, E2 and its third harmonic, B2, in the second bar, should tally.

Although this melody is also useful for checking the flute's scale, see Section 5 for more detailed experiments.

Check the octaves C♯2 and C♯3 by slurring from one to the other. As mentioned before in Section 1.2, sometimes the C♯3 is sharper or flatter than it should be due to either the head joint or the flute. If it is the head joint, it may be because the lip plate may be on a wider part of the tube. If it is the flute, then look at Section 5.1 for a solution to this.

J.S. Bach: 'Aus Liebe' from Passion According to St Matthew
Fig. 1.5

Bizet: 'Entr'acte' from Carmen
Fig. 1.6

ARTICULATION CHECKS

Finally, check both the flute and the head joint for their response to articulation. The two Dvořák symphony excerpts below will be a good start, following on with a section of Mendelssohn's 'Scherzo' from *A Midsummer Night's Dream*.

Dvořák: New World Symphony
Fig. 1.7

Mendelssohn: 'Scherzo' from A Midsummer Night's Dream
Fig. 1.8

TUBE THICKNESS

The thickness of the flute tube wall varies, but is broadly 0.014", 0.016" and 0.018", also known as 14, 16 or 18 thousandths of an inch in both gold and silver, though gold tubes are usually thinner because of their weight. Some makers produce in-between and other sizes too. I have tried several versions of each type and no solid conclusion could be made — only a preference. Different brands of flutes have also been tried over many years; some of the less-popular ones produce good instruments and, conversely, some of the top brands produce only moderately good flutes. Even some semi-student flutes are better than the professional models by the same manufacturer, which may seem strange. The bottom line is: *try it*. If it satisfies your criteria and the testing tunes above have been played with satisfactory results, then ask to have it on trial. It is not unreasonable to ask to try a flute for a week or so. Remember, there are so many variables that we can only conclude that a 'good' flute or head joint is the result of a formula which just happens to produce a pleasing result.

SEAMED TUBES

These became popular when 19th-century classic French flutes, made famous by Louis Lot, Bonneville, Lebret and others, were made available. They were made by rolling a precise width of sheet silver under pressure between two steel rollers, resulting in the formation of a tube. The edges then had to be hard-soldered together to make a flute tube. From the 1900s onwards, new methods of making seamless drawn tubes were made available and the practice of seamed tubes died out. However, into the 20th Century, seamed tubes were revived to satisfy the demands of the players of the classic French flutes. Nevertheless, there is no doubt that although the newly-made seamed-tube flutes had a character of their own, they really did not seem to match up to the characteristics of the original Lot flutes. Why this was so still remains a mystery, though there is no reason why a seamed tube should be any better than one without a seam. If a seam made such a difference, we should have seen players demanding that their favourite flutes be cut lengthways and soldered up again! The answer probably lies in the fact that the seamed tube flutes were older. Silver age-hardens, that is, it changes its structure over a long period of time. If a seam improves the flute, why not have a flute with several seams?

TUBE DIAMETER

This is traditionally 19mm (0.748") — a tiny amount under 3/4 of an inch. When Theobald Boehm first showed his newly-designed flute in 1847, he used millimetres, the common measure in Germany. If he had been British, he would have chosen 3/4 of an inch, about two thousandths of an inch larger than 19mm (0.748"). When a head joint won't fit snugly into a flute socket, it is because the socket was made to fit a different thickness of tube and not that the head joint is a 'wide bore' or 'narrow bore'. 99.9% of flutes are of a 19mm bore, but there are just a couple of makers who market c. 20mm (0.787") or 20.4mm (0.803") bore flutes. These are not widely-used at present. Widening the bore usually results in a sharper second octave — a problem recognised on larger flutes such as the alto and bass. This, in turn, makes clear articulation (especially staccato) more difficult.

MECHANISM COMFORT

Check the general 'feel' of the mechanism, though of course a new flute may feel strange for a time. The foot keys should be positioned in such a way to make it easy to access the lowest notes and to slide the right-hand pinkie.

The B♮ thumb key or lever (on the left hand) should be comfortable and angled in such a way that doesn't present a sharp edge to the thumb. This may not seem like a big deal, but after several hours of playing, this edge can become uncomfortable. Some manufacturers have designed a slanted rod-and-axle assembly which gives better long term reliability as the axle is longer. This idea, coupled with a comfortable thumb key, is worth more than a brief look.

Key extensions are available if the mechanism is uncomfortable in some way. Typical are extensions to the A key, the G key, and sometimes the left-hand C♯ key. Some flute makers will make extensions to order and a few flutists make them for their own flutes — these can often be glued on with an epoxy glue rather than soldered. Your repairperson should be able to advise you. A useful diagram of key names can be found at the beginning of the book.

MECHANISM HEIGHT

When a repairperson is completely overhauling and re-padding a flute, they may, in order to be helpful, set a lower height for the key cups above the tone holes. In experiments, it has been shown that lowering the key height to 'make playing faster and more comfortable' is a bad mistake as it flattens the pitch and slightly muffles the tone too. Ideally, it would be better to have no key cups at all, to allow complete venting, but as this is impracticable, the height of the cup and pad should be far enough above the tone hole to only minimally affect the tone or the pitch of that note.

As the cup is at an angle — more open at the front of the key than at the back — it is only practical to measure the key height from the front opening. For the foot joint key cups, a front opening of 4.5mm (0.177") is ideal. If this principal is continued into the right-hand keys, all is well and good, though a height of 4mm (0.157") would also be acceptable. For the left-hand key cups, a gap of 3.5mm (0.137") at the front is fine, though less than this and both the pitch and the tone will suffer.

It is advisable to seek the help of a repairperson if you want to change the height, as just removing cork from the tails of the keys is going to result in 'double action' — a clunky feel when two keys which lower together have not been set 'in sync'. The air column is said to vibrate above the tone hole in a curved-sided cone. Therefore, the centre of the key cup will have more effect on the pitch and tone.

FURTHER TUNING CHECKS

Some flutes have a sharp middle D. Check for this problem by playing the first interval in Fig. 1.9. If the D is too sharp, pull out the foot joint as much as the security of the socket will allow. If the socket is too loose, it would be wise to get it tightened for security. Next, check the second interval below. Most commonly, the D and the E♭ will be equally sharp, if at all. There is more on this problem in Section 5.1, *Check the tuning of your flute.*

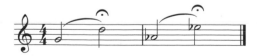

Fig. 1.9

Finally, play the few bars below to check that the flute and head joint produce octaves as they should (as mentioned in Section 1.3, *Choosing a flute*). An electronic tuner is helpful, though you should try to become accustomed to using your ear. The fourth bar uses the four harmonics of low C♯. Play this slurred to highlight any C♯ discrepancies. A more detailed test with suggestions on how to flatten a C♯ can be found in Section 5.1.

Fig. 1.10

1.4 HEAD JOINT AND FLUTE VARIABLES

DIMENSIONS

Below is a diagram of the common head joint dimensions, though each flute maker will have small variations on these.

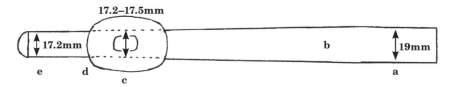

Head joint dimensions
Fig. 1.11

Notes to the diagram above: (a) The figure 19mm refers to the normal internal diameter of the flute tube. (b) This is the beginning of the taper. (c) This is the centre of the lip plate where the taper has reached between 17.2mm (0.677") and 17.5mm (0.688"). (d) and (e) A continuation of the taper — quite often a head joint straightens out for this last section, allowing the cork to be securely fitted in the cylindrical tube. From (b) to (c), most makers traditionally curve this contraction, as Boehm suggested, but a few makers make the contraction straight-sided. This is purely a manufacturer's preference, possibly because it is easier to produce.

In making a head joint tube, the process involves forcing a cylindrical tube to adopt the shape of a *mandrel*, a rod of hardened steel shaped to conform to the intended profile of the inside of the head joint. This forcing process will usually alter the metal thickness. Even when the tube is softened to allow it to re-shape, it cannot be forced to become *exactly* the same shape as the mandrel. Each tiny variable may affect the resulting tone and response, underlining the earlier statement that each head joint will be a little different from another.

The usual position for the centre of the lip plate is at the point at which the tube has contracted to 17.3mm (0.681"), though flute makers also differ with this, placing the lip plate centre from 17.2mm (0.677") to 17.5mm (0.688"). It may seem extraordinary to a performer, but this figure is significant. If the lip plate is placed on too wide a part of the tube, there may be difficulty playing octaves correctly in tune, especially C$\sharp_2$ and C$\sharp_3$.

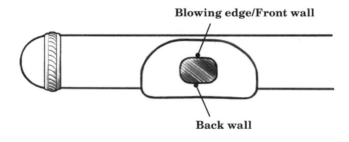

Blowing edge/Front wall

Back wall

Lip plate
Fig. 1.12

The short piece of vertical tube forming the blow hole in the lip plate is also known as the 'riser' or 'chimney'. The blow hole is about 12mm (0.47") long by 10mm (0.393") wide, though in recent years manufacturers have slightly reduced this to approximately 11.8mm (0.464") long by 9.8mm (0.385") wide, as this size seems to give a better projected tone. The size is not easy to see with the naked eye, as the edges of the embouchure hole are usually rounded off or overcut to help with articulation and the response of the lower notes. To measure it accurately, a Vernier gauge will be required, though a cheap plastic one would be accurate enough for this purpose. I have tried some head joints with holes up to 12.5mm long and 10.5mm wide, though the tone quality seemed to suffer when the limits were overstepped.

The front and back wall shapes, sizes and curves are common variables. The angle of difference from the vertical of the front wall is commonly 7°. The *depth* of the riser is measured at the sides of the embouchure hole which have the least height, and varies from about 4.8mm to 5.5mm. A deeper riser will favour the lower notes at the expense of the second and third octaves. If the riser is placed off-centre on the tube, that is, if it is placed in such a way as the front and back wall are of different depths, the head joint will give a variety of results depending on how far off-centre it is placed. If this is difficult to understand, just imagine the lip plate on the opposite page as being placed more towards the top of the diagram. This will force the maker to file (or undercut) the underside of the riser to make it fit the head joint tube.

Flute makers will try anything to get a better result, though after they have experimented with these variables — and we are considering adjustments of only tenths of millimetres — a lip plate, riser, and embouchure hole of standard sizes and heights tend to give the best results. The search for a louder and bigger sound has, in the past, resulted in experimenting with enlarging the embouchure hole, but after some time the size seemed not to help and flute makers returned to a slightly smaller size, as mentioned before, typically a fraction under both 10mm and 12mm.

Taken together, this information might be confusing to the reader. The easiest way to think of the head joint is that it is a formula where there are many variables. The internal shape, the metal used, the shape of the tube taper, whereabouts the lip plate is positioned, how the riser is placed, on what part of the tube the riser is positioned and all the other variables, each of which may affect the other, is why we should test a head joint very carefully for what it can do.

MATERIALS

It is only possible to advise about materials in a very general way. Precious metal flutes are available in a variety of materials and with an assortment of coatings, bondings, plating, fusing or cladding, making the choice difficult. Some flute makers use these terms, regardless of their meaning, to advertise their flutes in a manner which sounds like something a player must buy! As an aside and to add to the confusion, there are many fine wooden flutes too.

Flute makers are desperate to find new ways and new materials to attract customers. Since the first cylindrical Boehm flute of 1847 was introduced, there have been a number of variations upon the same theme — mixtures of metals are but one example. For instance, 'silver' can be 99% silver, or 95.8% silver, known as 'Brittania'; Sterling Silver is at 92.5%, and there are other recipes including 'Coin Silver' which vary from 90% to 80%, depending on the country of origin. Most flutes in the world are either US Coin Silver (at 90%) or Sterling Silver.

Similarly, gold can be found at 9 karat (pure gold is 24 karat and 9 karat is 9 parts in 24 of pure gold), 14, 18, 22 and even 24 karat, with some less common mixtures such as 15 karat. There are combinations of gold with other precious metals too, and flutes made of layers of silver and gold, rather like a sandwich. Note that 14 karat gold is only 58% pure gold — the remainder is copper or silver. Rose gold is standard gold with more copper than silver added.

What is important to us, the players, is that the flute makes a sound which pleases you and not its appearance or what it costs. Even more important is that the tone of your flute should be what your prospective employer and audience want to hear. Many believe that silver is the preferred material for most players due to its lower cost, ease of manufacturing, wider choice of instruments and perhaps its diversity of tone colour. Gold is a fine metal to try too, though there are far fewer choices available. Some makers mix silver and gold in both the flute body and head joint, and there are several other mixtures currently available. Remember to try out flutes using a head joint you are familiar with. A flute for life is one which suits you, talks to you and seems a part of your musical make-up. Gold or platinum are not better, neither is silver nor a mixture. There is a flute for each player and although this may change during your lifetime, choose what seems to work best for you.

Marcel Moyse played a silver-plated nickel-silver flute, a base metal with silver in its title because of its polished appearance, despite not containing any. He once commented,

> *'I prefer a flute without a built-in tone*
> *and then I can put into it what I want.'*

KEYWORK RELIABILITY

Hardened key work requires extra labour on the flute maker's part, but results in a more reliable instrument in the long term. Some flutes have soft keys, and the cup arms in particular may bend slightly with use. They may bend especially during assembly or when picking it up and putting it down the thousands of times that we do. This might put the cup and pad slightly out of alignment and cause a leak. A flute maker or repairperson should be able to tell you if the keys, especially the arms, have been hardened. It is also very important to remember that perfect padding is only possible on reliable, well-made and correctly-positioned key work. Note that finely-made key work, though frequently used, will last for several lifetimes and is usually quite easy to tighten up even when well worn.

Padding has also undergone changes in the past 50 years, though curiously we still rely on a circle of woven sheep's wool backed by cardboard and covered with what is described as a fish skin, but is in fact part of the lining of a cow's stomach. That, in the 21st Century! Plastic pads have been tried by some manufacturers, but the current opinion is still that the traditional pads, if properly fitted, are best. A competent and experienced repairperson is a must for the serious player, and inexperienced players should seek advice about such professionals.

DRAWN OR SOLDERED TONE HOLES

Soldered tone-hole chimneys were traditionally small sections of tube with the top edge shaped and carefully flattened to receive the pad. The bottom edge is filed in a curved shape to fit perfectly onto the flute's body. An examination of your own flute will help you to understand this process even if the tone holes are 'drawn'. Regardless of how the tone hole chimneys are made, they should not leak between the bottom edge of the chimney and the tube.

Drawn tone holes are pulled and spun out of the tube by using a special set of tools, one of which is wrapped around the tube and another is inserted inside the bore. The tone holes are therefore part of the tube itself, but since this process draws metal from the tube, it may alter the tube's thickness and some believe this affects the tone. However, drawn tone holes are leak-proof, whereas soldered tone holes may show signs of leaks after many years of use, especially where water collects around the trill, thumb, and G♯ holes. The use of better solders, plus over-plating after all the soldering work has been done, has minimised this problem in recent years. The general opinion seems to be that soldered holes are a better option at present, based purely on tonal considerations. Some flute makers solder just one or two holes onto an otherwise drawn tone hole flute. This is to simplify the manufacturing process and perhaps to affect the tuning of a particular note.

OPEN-HOLE CUPS (FRENCH-STYLE)

These give the player access to contemporary techniques and special fingerings. For example, *multiphonics* and *glissandos* throughout most of the instrument are made possible. Several contemporary pieces require quarter tones, which are far easier to execute with open cups. A further consideration may be that with a flute with intonation problems, the open cups provide a way of slightly modifying the pitch and tuning of some notes. That said, open-hole or 'French-style' flutes are no better tone-wise than a correctly set up, closed-hole flute. 'Correctly set up' because closed-hole flutes often have the key cups closer to the tone holes, dulling the tone and flattening the pitch a little, as explained in Section 1.3, *Mechanism height*. Why closed-holed flutes are more prone to this problem is not known. On both open- and closed-hole flutes, perhaps repairpeople lower the cups to make the playing of technical passages smoother, as the key cups are closer to the tone holes.

The origin of open cups was an attempt by French players to encourage a better hand position. It was thought that the new Boehm system flutes might have a wider appeal if they had open cups, similar to the ring keys on old simple-system flutes. Some players also felt that direct contact with the open holes gave them greater control too. Some even say that open-hole flutes have a more 'open' tone, perhaps rounder and with less pronounced harmonics. However, this is contrary to common sense: there are 13 fundamental notes on the flute and only five of these have open cups, yet this does not suggest that there are five good notes and seven bad ones!

For the newcomer to open-hole flutes, changing over takes but a few days and with a little willpower. Plugging one or more open holes must only be considered as a purely temporary measure, as the plug will flatten the pitch of the note as if the tone hole has been moved further down the tube by more than 1mm.

The player might consider using a closed-hole flute if they have very thin fingers, or if they have problems keeping their fingertips smooth — rough fingertips can cause small leaks. I have proved this theory by experimenting with an air-operated pressure tool to measure air escaping from a poorly-set-up pad. On an open-hole flute, the fingertips were tested first with roughened skin (after gardening) and then again with domestic cling film wrapped around the fingertip. There was a difference in response — the cling-film-wrapped finger proved leak-proof. Anyone who has gardener's fingers will also experience a slight loss of power from leaky fingers, especially at rose-pruning time!

Those with small fingers can generally cope with an open-hole flute. It is not just the finger width which determines covering the hole, but the stretch between the fingers. Additionally, it is not only the distance between the third and fourth fingers but the distance between all fingers which, if increased, leads to a more relaxed hand position. With some players, their fingers not only rise and fall but move sideways as well, in order to cover a hole — an action which can prevent the player from executing a rapid technique. Use a mirror to see if you have this problem. To overcome this, stretch your fingers on the right-angled edge of some furniture. Do it often. In time, it will help to overcome the sideways movement and will increase the speed of technique. Just a few seconds several times a day will do it. A piano is ideal for this purpose, and you may have observed pianists doing this exercise to increase their finger stretch for large intervals.

EXTRA KEYS

Most players manage without much extra key work, holding the view that there is more to go wrong. However, with modern mechanisms, failure is far less likely than with older flutes. There are some key work additions which will make life easier.

Gizmo: this so-called 'gizmo' key is found on the foot joint and pushes down the low B_1 cup separately to sound C_4. It is an option on flutes with a low B foot and can be useful, though there are fingerings which allow this note to sound well without this additional key. That said, there are occasions when the 'gizmo' can assist in making other notes more resonant when used in slow passages.

Lower G insert: This is a metal insert placed inside the lower G key tone hole (arrowed below) to help facilitate E_3 without fitting a split-E mechanism. This insert takes different forms, varying from a donut shape to a half-moon shape. Both do help to make top E easier, but the unfortunate downside is that they result in a poor, fuzzy-sounding tone on A_1 and A_2, and (more seriously), make both these notes flat too, especially the donut. The insert is better removed and can be simply pushed out after removing the mechanism, as it is normally just glued in. If you paid to have one put in, take it out, and put it down to experience and thank your lucky stars you have acquired two better A naturals!

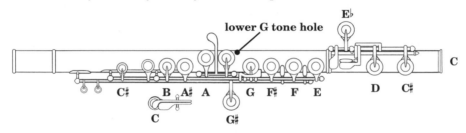

Location of lower G tone hole
Fig. 1.13

Split-E mechanism: This is an extra arm attached to the right-hand mechanism so that when the second finger is pressed, the lower G tone hole, arrowed above, is closed. This also means altering the mechanism of the left-hand third finger so that the two cups are independent.

Split-E clutch: This is a locking device which can either allow use of the split-E mechanism or disable it. It is in the form of a small bolt attached to the G key and extends sideways to the key arrowed above. It is another option, though those who have one report that they rarely use it.

Convertible B/C foot joint: This makes it possible to have both foot joints in one design. It seems an unnecessary expense and a carefully chosen flute, either with a B or C foot, is usually adequate for most jobs. Some players use a C foot and have a spare B foot for use when required. For many years, players around the world managed with a piece of cigar tube, 19mm in diameter, placed in the end of the C foot. Any suitable piece of tube will do the trick, though when used for low B_1, C_1 becomes unavailable.

G/A mechanism: On a flute where this has been fitted, some players have observed that the instrument is a little less responsive when compared to a flute without this key. The reason why is unknown, but one possible explanation is that the extra hole (or pad) interferes in some way with the acoustic response. In the diagram on the next page, the placement of the key is shown in bold, though the exact position of the key is a matter of preference by each maker. The touch piece, operated by the right hand, is placed next to the first trill key. It opens two holes, one just below the thumb key and one above, next to the trill keys. Its advantage is that it facilitates the high G/A trill. There are fingerings which, with practice, can be used just as effectively, though not as easily.

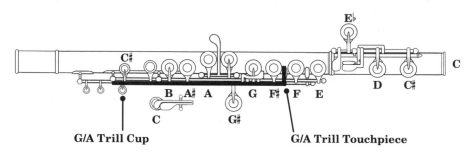

G/A trill mechanism
Fig. 1.14

C♯ trill: This is a large cup placed next to the thumb hole of the C₂ key shown below. It is designed to help the player trill easily from B to C♯ and from C to C♯ and also on a high G♯. Note that both trills are readily available without this option and with a little practice. When I tested several flutes by the same manufacturer over a period of time, I found the flutes without the extra key to be more responsive, though the reasons are unknown.

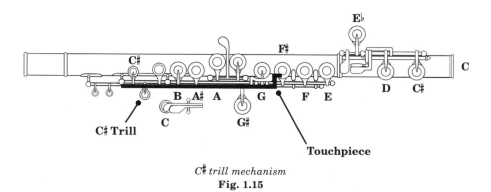

C♯ trill mechanism
Fig. 1.15

This key also enables several other useful trills to be played: B to C♯, C to C♯, F♯3 to C♯3, G3 to A♭3, G3 to A3, A♭3 to B♭3 using the trill and finger. It is also useful for improving the tone quality of A♭3 and C♯2. Those who have one will know there are many uses for this key.

An extra roller: Added to the low E♭ key, this allows an easier slide for the pinkie from E♭ to C♯ and vice versa. One added to the low C♯ key will also allow a slide onto the C key, and vice versa. Some makers shape or offset these keys at an angle to facilitate these slides and make for an easier movement of the little finger.

Engraved lip plate: This is a very good idea as it helps stabilise the lip plate on your lip in hot conditions. You can achieve the same effect within a few moments without engraving by following the instructions in Section 1.5, *Lip plate insecurity*.

Offset G♯: This is when the G♯ cup under the flute has been angled to slightly raise it above the line where moisture can gather and obstruct the hole. It can easily be seen — it is a diagonal arm to the key cup rather than a straight up-and-down arm. It adds strength to the key and avoids the trill key tubing.

Angled thumb keys: These too can be easily seen, as the rod and sleeve with the axle holding the keys in place is diagonally angled. This is to provide a steady action and less likely to become unstable or suffer from wear. Another good idea.

D foot: The C foot was an extension introduced around 1765. Before this time, D1 was the lowest note. Some manufacturers give an option for an extra foot which only has one key, the D♯ key. I made several of these in the 1970s for use in performing 18th-century music, and it certainly made a big difference to the second octave, allowing it to sing out, loud and clear. However, the tone quality is different and it is advisable to first check the response of your flute before ordering one. I have more recently made a C♯ foot too, where the lowest note is C♯1, seen below.

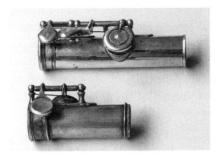

D foot and C♯ foot
Fig. 1.16

The vented left-hand C♯ key: There are various experiments taking place as I write, to address the lack of colour of C♯2. These range from testing different-sized holes, the C♯ key placement and even a double-key arrangement. During the next few years, there will no doubt be improvements that are worth looking out for. Already, there is a 'vented C key' for the piccolo, which is a small hole in the left-hand first finger key, usually called the C♯ key. There are various claims that it improves E2 and helps the intonation of some third-octave notes.

INLINE/OFFSET FLUTES

Inline flutes were originally made for an easier manufacturing process. Some 19th-century players also felt that the tone holes should be placed in a straight line down the flute for acoustic reasons, ignoring the fact that there are several, including the foot-joint tone holes, which are not. It was also felt that inline keys encouraged a better left-hand position. The theory was that with the left-hand first finger tucked well under the flute to support it, the left-hand third finger can be more comfortably placed centrally on the G key. This can work for most players, though some are likely to have problems in time because the wrist is too sharply angled. An offset G flute is much preferred, both for comfort and reliability of the mechanism. It allows a comfortable left-hand position and rarely creates problems later in life. Ask any repairperson for their views about repairing a flute with inline or offset keys.

If you have an inline flute, check the reliability of the key labelled B in the diagram at the beginning of this book and its supporting rod by playing F3 and slurring to F♯3. Usually, there is no problem here. With some tension, perhaps due to the stress of performing these two notes as part of a solo in a symphony, the second note may not always sound. This is because pressure on the A♯ cup then puts pressure on its supporting rod, which is on the same axle as the B key — the key which needs to rise to sound F♯3. Do note that you may not experience this problem on a well-maintained flute, but it may occur as a flute becomes worn or is not in good working order. It is extraordinary that this problem is more likely to occur when the hall, the player and the flute are all hot.

1.5 CUSTOMISING YOUR FLUTE

ALTERING THE TRILL KEY

There are occasions when a note may need help in maintaining pitch in *pianissimo* or *diminuendo*. An example is E♭2 when playing the final four bars of the second movement of C.P.E. Bach's *Sonata in G Minor* (attrib. to J.S. Bach), shown below.

Excerpt from the second movement of C.P.E. Bach's Sonata in G Minor: gradually put a little pressure on the second trill key in the final two or three bars.
Fig. 1.18

The exceptionally long E♭2 is not easy to manage in *diminuendo* without becoming flat. Using the first trill key can help to maintain the intonation. Slightly lean on this key with the right-hand first finger whilst playing the E♭. Do this in such a way that opens the trill key a fraction, without fully pressing it down. Note that on an open-hole flute, you can also subtly uncover a small portion of the vent in the cup. To make this easier in the future, and to use this for other notes, the trill key touchpiece should be bent slightly towards the F key. How much depends on the positioning of the key between the two cups and the width of your finger. If it is bent too much, it may be pressed inadvertently during other passage work. Ask your repairperson to do this for you with a pair of 'parallel pliers'. The trill key can also be added at the end of a *diminuendo* on both E♭3 and E3, though care is needed as these are normally sharp notes and adding the trill key will make them sharper still and may need flattening.

Similarly, the second trill key can be gently pressed when playing a *pianissimo* F2, particularly in *diminuendo*.

LIP PLATE INSECURITY

Some manufacturers used to engrave the lip plate with flowers or their monogram to make the lip plate less slippery for the lower lip. Why this isn't common now is a mystery, as there are many of us who have, at some point, suffered from a sweaty and slippery lip plate on a concert platform with strong lights. This problem is easy to fix and can be done by sticking a small section of the non-printed edging of a sheet of stamps where the lower lip is placed. Some players use an entire stamp, though this is not recommended as the ink can transfer onto skin if it gets moist. The blank edge, with no ink, is safer. There are custom-made stickers which will also do the job, though if the paper is used for too long a period and it becomes dirty, there is a risk of a lip infection.

A semi-permanent solution is to 'frost' the lip plate which is, in effect, to make minute scratches on it to provide grip. Enquire in a good hardware or engineering shop for either the finest grade of carborundum or crocus paper. The latter is a fine jeweller's sandpaper used for removing minor marks on precious metals. First, place a strip of tape across the lip plate (as shown in Fig. 1.19) to protect the embouchure hole, then lightly rub the crocus paper on the lower part of the lip plate. This will 'frost' the silver, giving it security and grip when your chin perspires. It causes no harm and the frosting can easily be removed by a repairperson, or by energetic rubbing with a silver cloth and some metal polish. Take care here if the lip plate is plated, as too much rubbing with crocus paper may remove some plating. A solid head joint will be quite safe.

Lip plate with tape
Fig. 1.19

A small piece of paper (such as a postage stamp) stuck to the flute where the left-hand first finger joint is usually placed on the flute body will also add extra security to the lips, though if this still doesn't fix the problem then a thin piece of cork glued here will do the job even better. Any proprietary glue will be fine to use, though the traditional 'shellac' glue (which is similar to varnish) is also fine. A small, round, self-adhesive corn plaster will do the trick too. If any of the previously mentioned products need to be removed later, surgical spirit or rubbing alcohol will remove any residue and cause no harm.

If security is still an issue, be sure your right-hand little finger is being placed on the E♭ key when moving from C♯2 to D2 and E2. If the little finger is not placed correctly, it will add to insecurity and may cause the flute to wobble.

THE ROCKSTRO POSITION

If the above solutions haven't fixed the insecurity, the problem might be due to posture and possibly to the connection of your flute with the head joint. This was looked at in some detail in the 19th Century by Richard S. Rockstro (1826–1906), a flutist and teacher. The 'Rockstro Position', as it has been termed in recent years, refers to a particular correlation between the head joint, the main body of the flute and the flutist, which allows the flute to rest on the first joint of the left-hand first finger, rather than the flute pushed against the chin. The result is a more relaxed left hand and, more importantly, it should help to avoid tension and possible muscular problems in later years. Remember that younger players can easily employ a poor playing position without any feeling of discomfort, but it is only later in life that problems may occur when the muscles and tendons are less forgiving.

Marcel Moyse, the celebrated soloist, asked the Couesnon flute makers of Paris in the 1930s to make him a flute with extensions to the left-hand second and third fingers, as shown below.

Couesnon flute: left-hand mechanism
Fig. 1.20

In recent times, players have looked again at Rockstro's work and some have adopted the Rockstro position. In the latter part of the 19th Century, when the Boehm flute was becoming more widely used, players were advised to keep the keys in line with the centre of the lip plate. This results in tucking the index finger of the left hand underneath the flute, supporting it from below. Rockstro's alternative was to turn the flute body outwards, leaving the lip plate in its customary position on the mouth. The outcome is that the flute body now *rests* on the index finger and reduces the need to push the flute hard against the chin. The precise amount that you turn out the flute body is your choice, but a little less than half an inch (about 10mm) in circumference should be enough. It will take some practice to get accustomed to it, but the result will be a secure embouchure and an easier movement of the left-hand third finger, especially on an inline flute. To consider adopting this position, you can make the change in a few small steps. In relation to the head joint, turn the body of the flute outwards by about 1/4 inch. The right-hand fingers now need to curve a little more over the flute, but the *left-hand index finger* does not need to bend under the flute quite so much.

If you decide, after experimenting, that you want to change to the Rockstro position, place a marker using nail polish or a permanent marker pen where the head joint meets the socket, to remind yourself where to place the head joint in daily practice.

If you experience any tension or hurt in your teens or early twenties, this is more likely to get worse as the years advance. It is wiser to change now. I knew a London professional player who adopted the Rockstro position to the degree where the right-hand keys were at right angles to the head joint, that is, with the key work facing outwards! He had a long and distinguished career.

Finally, clean the tenon of the head joint (the part which slides into the socket) with a cloth which has been dipped in rubbing alcohol and clean the inside of the socket too. This will allow easy adjustment during practice.

OPEN-HOLE DIFFICULTIES: LEFT HAND

Left-hand problems usually occur on flutes with an inline mechanism, and involve difficulties with covering the third-finger tone hole sufficiently well. This can be observed not only visually, but can be also be heard as a minute *glissando* when slurring between G and A. Consider modifying your hand position by changing to the 'Rockstro' position, outlined above. This is even more of a problem for those with narrow or small fingers. The long-term solution is to have an offset G flute, or change to a closed-hole flute. If a custom-made flute is ordered, a knowledgeable flute manufacturer can make the left-hand third finger tone hole as a closed cup, but should be placed 1mm higher, or 'north'. This is because changing an open cup to a closed cup, or plugging the hole, will flatten the note beneath. (See Section 5.1, *Flute scales*.)

Some players experience problems with the left-hand first finger when gripping the flute too tightly and can cause the finger to tingle, or become numb and turn white. These are all indicators of lack of blood supply to the finger. To relieve this pressure, place a circular self-adhesive corn plaster at the point where the finger is positioned on the flute body and the problem should be resolved. If the problem persists, use two plasters, one on top of the other, or consider using some soft but firm foam stuck to the flute with double-sided sticky tape. There are commercial add-ons which also address this problem, available at flute shops.

OPEN-HOLE DIFFICULTIES: RIGHT HAND

There is no reason acoustically not to have a mixture of open and closed holes, as has been done with Brannen's 'Orchestral Model', a design suggested by Albert Cooper. It has open cups on the right hand only, because those in the left hand are the least useful. Of course, a player might plug the left-hand holes on their open-hole flute, but note that plugging these will flatten the A and A♯s in both octaves — not a sensible idea.

FOOT KEY PROBLEMS

If you are unable to get to the lowest notes easily, there may be several reasons why. Get the flute checked out for leaks, not so much in the foot joint itself but in the main body of the flute from G downwards. Be sure that the foot joint is also securely fitted to its tenon. Some leak-testing procedures can be found in Section 5.4, *Checking the mechanism* and *Leaky pads*.

The main cause for foot keys leaking is the frequent removing and assembly of the foot joint which, over time, can result in a slight bending of the foot keys. This may cause leaks where the pads and tone holes meet. After a while, these small stresses add up. To check, look at the foot keys whilst gently pressing down the low C♮ roller, *not the key cup*. If the C♯ key goes down exactly with the C♮ cup then all should be well. If not, it will need the services of your repairperson, and you will need to take more care in future when fitting your foot joint.

A good tip is to always twist the joint in one direction so that the joints wear more evenly. Be sure the two parts are parallel to each other, and hold down the keys when assembling.

FOOT JOINT INSECURITY

If there are still problems using the foot keys E♭, C♯, C and B effectively, the problem is most often a right-hand position which leans too much to the left. The solution is unfortunately not a short-term fix and may take about a month to resolve. It involves changing your hand position in such a way that the right hand leans the opposite way — to the *right*. This will feel awkward for some days, perhaps very awkward. At the same time, the right-hand thumb should be moved a little to the right under the flute, which will help to ease the tension. A circular corn plaster stuck under the flute will serve as a reminder of where the right-hand thumb should be placed. This change in hand position will require much patience and slow practice for a time, but once mastered it will lead to greater flexibility and agility with the foot keys. I have advised students many times that this 'lean to the right' correction should be exaggerated for a week or so, and then relaxed for the next month. This seems to produce a better, longer-term result. Older players, around or over the age of 30, are best advised not to change their hand position without advice as this may cause undue tension in the hand, arm or shoulders. Their bodies are less forgiving!

If the foot keys seem to be difficult or ineffective to use, have the foot checked for leaks as suggested in Section 5.4, *Leaky pads*, onwards. It needs to be well adjusted to be efficient.

When you have trouble sliding from the E♭ key to the low C or C♯ key and back in tricky passagework, the solution is to either obtain a silicone spray available from a hardware shop or to obtain a small container of graphite powder (used for easing door locks). For the former, spray a tiny amount of silicone onto a piece of card and lightly touch the sprayed surface with the tip of your right-hand little finger. Then, wipe your finger on a clean piece of paper — the finger should have picked up enough to make sliding easy. For the graphite powder, take care! It is usually in a 'puffer' container and you only need a tiny amount — if you squeeze the pack too vigorously, you will get black graphite powder everywhere! A similar result can be obtained by rubbing a very soft leaded pencil (4B works well) on a piece of paper or the surface tip of your little finger. The effect will last most of the day, unless you wash your hands. Alternatively, as most professional players do, you can run your little finger over an oily part of your face, usually the side of your nose or forehead, to help it slide. This will need to be done immediately prior to playing the difficult passage.

Another tip is to stick small 'buttons' of foam to the inside of the lid of your flute case. They will correspond with the lowest two or three foot joint keys (C#, C and B) when the case is closed, and should hold the keys *very gently* shut so that an impression is made on the pad. This will also make your life easier for the lowest notes!

DENTS

Contrary to popular belief, small dents in the flute's tubing seem to have little or no effect on the tone and are no more influential than droplets of water commonly found in the tube during playing. If you have small dents, don't worry about them, unless you are buying the flute second-hand, in which case you can beat the price down!

1.6 THE PICCOLO

THE PICCOLO

Players are sometimes unaware that almost all professional piccolos have a conical body and cylindrical head, unlike the flute with its conical head and cylindrical body. However, there *are* cylindrical-bodied piccolos and it is generally agreed that the tone of these is inferior, though the third octave and extreme upper notes are much easier to play. Some professional players have both models and use the cylinder model for particularly difficult upper-register work. Some also have a D♭

piccolo — a semitone higher than usual — for use in, for example, the solo in Tchaikovsky's *Fourth Symphony*. It allows the player to finger it a semitone lower — a much easier key.

On many piccolos, the middle E♭ and D are sharp compared to the rest of the scale. The lowest note on a piccolo is usually D, which is easy to flatten by placing a small amount of filler such as *plasticene* or *playdough* in the end so that it covers about 1/6th of the open end. The E♭ can be similarly flattened by removing the key used by the little finger and placing a small amount of filler at the 'north' end (nearest the head) of the hole so that the air has to travel further before exiting, thus flattening the E♭. Only a small amount is required to be effective. The reason why these two notes are sharp isn't known, but it could be because the bore of the conical piccolo flares out just before the E♭ hole to the very end of the tube and the D hole. The amount of 'flare' in the last inch or so of the bore may have been copied from various makers and perhaps overdone, thus sharpening these two notes. The flare can easily be seen by looking up the bore from the end of the tube.

There are piccolos with a low C, a note called for only very occasionally, and even more recently there are piccolos which descend to low B. These may be worth a look as the extra length usually affects the availability of some upper notes and may affect the tone of the rest of the range. The extra keys might not be used for playing these low notes, but could be useful for tempering and varying the response of upper notes, and (as on the flute) used for playing very softly.

Choosing a piccolo needs some skill as there are many features to check besides choosing wood or metal. If you about to purchase a piccolo, do first try to practice one for a few weeks to become accustomed to its demands. It will be much easier to decide after this experience.

I remember watching the piccolo player in a Russian ballet orchestra in 2015 who *never* made an entry without a habitual, quick, gentle blow at the thumb holes, trill keys and G♯ holes to be sure no water blocked the holes. This was done in a matter of seconds. It was an impressive and sensible strategy.

1.7 TRANSPORTING FLUTES

SECURITY

Those who travel must be aware that thieves are on the lookout for smart gear. Your costly leather flute case proclaims *'I'm carrying something expensive'*. If carrying a flute through a doubtful city area, I carry mine in a supermarket grocery bag.

A thief is also on the lookout for people whose attention is diverted. I once saw one at a train station, cutting through the leather strap of a shoulder bag with hi-tech snips and running off with it at high speed. It took less than a couple of seconds to complete the job.

Always carry valuable items in front of your body when in risky situations, and carry them in an inexpensive bag. Don't put a bag down in a public place, as thieves are well practised in grabbing and running. The most common scenario is the traveller placing a bag on the floor either while using a phone, or occupied buying something at a kiosk.

A gift for the thief is a backpack with a flute case poking out of the top. It takes but a second to grab the flute and run.

Never leave a flute in a car or in the trunk, even when locked. Anyone who does that, even for a shortest time, deserves little sympathy if something happens to it.

MAILING A FLUTE

There are two main considerations: stopping the flute from moving around in the case, and having sufficient soft material wrapped around the outside to cushion the flute and its case from bumps. If there is space inside the case, use bubble wrap or another material to prevent the flute parts from moving around. Putting a strip between the joints and over the keys will have the same effect.

When labelling, if the parcel is sufficiently well packed, a 'FRAGILE' label may be unnecessary and may even attract trouble. Some workers in the trade say that a 'FRAGILE' notice invites a rogue worker to throw a parcel about, so this may make matters worse.

Special protective flute cases can also be obtained for mailing purposes.

TRAVELLING BY AIR

At larger airports, security staff are fairly accustomed to seeing flutes. The usual procedure is for nothing to happen, though you may be asked to open the case so they can take a look. It is, however, rare for them to ask for the flute to be taken out of the case. Even if the security staff wish to handle the flute, they customarily do so with care. The only time they ask to check your flute and other belongings is if you behave in a bristly way which leads them to suspect you may be carrying more than a flute. Or, being human, they may wish to make it equally awkward for you! I have travelled for 40 years with several flutes in a standard but internally-modified foam-filled carry-on bag, which is almost never opened. A good point to remember when passing through the security checks is to answer questions simply and politely and — most importantly — don't talk or make jokes about dangerous items or security scenarios!

In recent years, some flute materials have been restricted from crossing borders, such as ivory, and more recently what are known as 'precious woods', such as rosewood. A CITES licence may be required for travelling with flutes made from these materials. CITES — the Convention on International Trade in Endangered Species (of Wild Fauna and Flora) — is an international agreement between governments. Its aim is to ensure that international trade in specimens of wild animals and plants does not threaten their survival. You can find information about such licences online.

2

Section 2
Educational Assistance

2.1 PRACTISING

WHAT TO PRACTISE

A sensible practice routine should include exercises to address specific weaknesses, as well as the practice of orchestral audition excerpts, to help your employability. The time spent on them may vary, depending on the problems of the player. What will work best is if you write down your plan and the amount of time you should spend on each item. A suggested daily plan is set out here.

- A short warm-up; adding 'patterns' in all keys as in the Reichert 'Daily Exercise No. 2' as in Fig. 2.11. *5 minutes.*

- Tone exercises. *20 minutes.*

- Finger exercises as set out in Section 2.3, *Finger exercises. 25 minutes.*

- Scales and arpeggios. *20 minutes.*

- Special problems (articulation, vibrato, intonation, etc. *5–10 minutes, or more as necessary.*

- Studies. *30 minutes.*

- The flute literature; a popular piece from the repertoire. *15 minutes.*

- Melodies. *10 minutes.*

- The piccolo. *10 minutes.*

- The orchestral repertoire; the 30 most popular audition excerpts, such as Debussy's *Prélude à l'après-midi*, Mendelssohn's 'Scherzo', Bach's 'Aus Liebe', Rossini's 'Overtures', etc. A list of the *Top 28* can be found in *An Orchestral Practice Book, Vol. 1. 15 minutes.*

Total: *about 2 hours and 30 minutes.*

An ambitious student at a music school would spend more time than this and a university or other college student who has several other commitments might have to cut down on this schedule on some days.

For a serious contender for an orchestral position, the time spent on some of these categories should be increased.

2.2 PRACTICE SCHEDULES

A ONE-YEAR PRACTICE PLAN

First, know your personal weaknesses and playing problems. If you are not sure, ask another player or try to remember what your teacher most often mentioned needed to be worked on; it is those problems which need the most practice. To get the better of them, make a *practice plan* of about one year in length. This is the most effective way of getting good, fast, especially if you remember to look for exercises which help to fix your playing problems — or even make up your own!

- Include three one-week breaks in your plan to have a rest from playing — this is important to refresh and reinvigorate your enthusiasm.

- There are other practice schedules and ideas set out in my book *Looking at More Efficient Practice* for different levels of achievement. Find your preference and then make your plan.

- Set yourself a goal to learn at least one new repertoire piece each month. Make a list and tick them off as you learn them.

REGULARITY

Practising regularly will yield the best results, of course, but practising at the same time each day is even more beneficial, though not always possible. To squeeze a little more out of your practice time, do the same type of exercise at the *same time* each day, such as technical and finger exercises, tone exercises, scales and studies. It seems that we progress faster when we behave like a machine. Why this works so well is not known, but it just does. If the discipline of regular practice is a problem, develop a better habit by practising a routine each day for two weeks. Once this regularity is established, it should be easier to continue. Those first two weeks will need determination, discipline and resolve to keep going.

If possible, your plan should also include the occasional practice of improvisation and the practice of melodies. (Investigate the selection of 72 bass lines in *Efficient Practice*.) If there are serious deficiencies in technique (taking into consideration your age and aspirations) then two technical sessions a day may be necessary, though take care not to overdo it and cause strain. If two such sessions are needed, they should be widely separated by about 6–8 hours. Articulation is best done in several short sessions each day for a few minutes, because the tongue gets tired.

A two-week time limit is best imposed on etudes or studies, because after regular daily work it might be better to say 'I have not finished with you, but I'll see you later!'. Regularity is most definitely the best way to improve articulation.

2.3 TONE

TONE — WARMING UP

Always warm the tube before playing, as it will respond better and the tone will sound better. Use a slow movement of air through the tube as if you were sighing. Some players habitually warm up, even on stage, by blowing a rush of wind down the tube. This is inefficient, besides being noisy and insensitive, and can offend a jury or an audition panel. It is, however, a useful contemporary technique called a *jet whistle*, and should only be used for that purpose.

Some easy sequences are useful to start a successful practice session. For example, an exceptional exercise is No. 2 of Reichert's *7 Daily Exercises*. It can also be found in the compilation *Complete Daily Exercises*. Play it slowly to start with, in an easy key, modulating into a few other keys before continuing seamlessly into other tone exercises.

TUNING UP

This is important, even if you are playing alone, as you need to accustom your ear to an identical pitch each day. Of course, fine tuning is necessary when playing with others, but tune up during practice so that intonation problems are revealed and corrected, and *expressive intonation* is more easily achieved. After a time, your pitch will become stable, at least at the same temperature, so the tuning procedure will be faster. Use the instructions for checking the pitch of your flute as outlined in Section 5.1, *Check the tuning of your flute*.

The amount that the head joint is pulled out should be about the same every day, though this may need adjusting when the temperature is unusually high or low. It is important to play at the same pitch daily, so you become more aware of and able to correct any pitch problems. Almost all flutes are made to have the head pulled out by around 0.5cm (or 0.22") or more. The cork is fully discussed in Section 5.4, *The head joint and cork*. It is worth noting that some experienced players believe that the tiny extra space in the socket made by pulling out the head actually improves the tone slightly.

Curiously, the flute itself will improve in time — if it is played daily with a good tone and the harmonics are in agreement with the fundamental (see Section 5.1, *Flute scales* and 5.1, *Check the tuning of your flute*). Why this is true is not known, but other instrumentalists say the same thing. I have played flutes which have undoubtedly been played well and even allowed for the identification of the player. It is not hard to tell if a frequently-used flute has been played imperfectly or well.

TONE EXERCISES

Perhaps a more sensible approach may be to practise tone *colour* exercises. Playing long tones can achieve a great deal as they allow us to listen carefully for defects, and correct them. When working on a specific goal, progress is likely to be faster with a precise objective in mind. It is the *colour of the tone* which is best worked on.

What influences a player's tone? No doubt, the physical make-up of a player lends itself to a certain tone, and when that tone is beautiful from the outset we say these people have a 'natural talent' or gift. Most of us simply have to work hard at it.

There are many variables which make up tone. These can be seen as part of a 'recipe', elements of which have an influence on the tone's character and colour. Amongst these are the size of the mouth cavity, the nasal cavity, the throat shape, the size and shape of the lips, the aperture between the lips, the angle of the air and its speed… and, as mentioned before, perhaps the body size of the player has an influence too. Of course, the flute and head joint are also influential. Some of these physical attributes, such as the angle of the air and the mouth cavity, can be modified during practice and greatly affect the tone.

It is certainly more beneficial to work on a particular colour because you will need a palette of colours to choose from when you play expressively. The flute is capable of large colour differences, much more than other woodwinds, and we should take every advantage of this attribute.

Yellow Colour The soft and hollow flute sound has weak harmonics and it can be described as a 'yellow' tone as opposed to the richer, darker 'purple' tone we hear with its stronger harmonics. The yellow tone should be the basic colour to start off tone exercises with because it contains the biggest proportion of *fundamental* or *first harmonic*. To understand this better, think of a jug full of tone… The fundamental is the lowest note and has no strong colour because it has no harmonics — we can refer to it as *yellow* or *pure*. Adding harmonics in different proportions adds more colour, though the tone jug is not limitless — the flute only has about five harmonics that we can play with. If the performer chooses to play with a *hard* or *purple* tone, this will make the upper harmonics louder, *usually at the expense of the fundamental*. The bigger the proportion of fundamental, the more the tone will project. This might seem surprising, but the hollow tone projects more because lower frequencies travel greater distances than higher ones. (A ship in foggy weather sounds a low-pitched foghorn so that its sound travels the greatest distance.) Check your yellow tone in the Fauré *Pavane* below, which requires a soft, hollow and projecting tone.

Fauré: Pavane, Op. 50
Fig. 2.1

How the harmonics in a tone affect the sound we hear is best illustrated by the oboe and violin on their lower notes. Both have around 12 or 13 harmonics in their sound and, although slightly similar, the listener can tell them apart by the *relative strength of those harmonics*. They have the same ingredients, but are made up from a different recipe.

If possible, do your tone practice in a room which neither flatters nor makes you sound bland or breathy.

Begin your tone exercise with A1 or G1 and find your best tone. Then, very slightly, begin altering each of the following variables in turn. Don't rush!

- Your mouth shape (by opening your teeth a little)

- Very slightly yawning and relaxing (to alter the throat cavity)

- The shape of your lips (the aperture between them)

- The angle of the air stream

- The air speed

- The amount you cover the embouchure hole with your lower lip

The latter has a significant influence on the size and quality of the tone, as well as its pitch.

Next, begin the melody below (Saint-Saëns: 'The Aquarium'). Try to sustain the same soft and pure colour down to low D. Sometimes, this will sound with a different colour to the A and G♯. Use the experiments above to help keep the same colour.

Saint-Saëns: 'The Aquarium' from The Carnival of the Animals
Fig. 2.2

If these experiments are done daily, you should soon find the best embouchure to create your most beautiful 'yellow' tone. The second part of 'The Aquarium' (from the fifth bar) will help you achieve the same tone colour from A1 down to E1 as it descends by small steps rather than in fifths. These smaller steps help to detect tone changes more easily.

Purple Colour After a week or two of trying to perfect a pure yellow tone, move on to the richer *purple* colour. At this point, the objective is to play with two colours, each as different as possible: the yellow tone with a stronger fundamental and the purple tone with stronger harmonics. In achieving this, it can be seen that your own distinctive tone must lie somewhere in between these two extremes. To achieve the purple tone colour, the air stream should be directed more downwards than across — the exact amount can only be discovered by experiment. When directing the air further downward, it is *essential* not to cover the embouchure hole by turning the head joint in on your lip. Covering more of the hole will make the tone 'harder' but will also flatten the pitch.

The low register from D_1 up to C_2 is the best place to begin because these are the fundamental notes of the instrument. Only when the harmonics are sounding in tune with the fundamental (easier said than done) should you move into the second octave. The way to do this is to listen to yourself and try to detect the faint harmonics. If necessary, overblow into the harmonic series to see if they are in tune with the fundamental. See Section 5, *Ear training, playing in tune*. This details a process which will improve your ability to hear more in your tone.

After training your ear, you might be more aware of at least one or two of the harmonics you are producing within your low-register notes, especially when playing with a hollow yellow tone rather than a rich and buzzy purple one. This personal ear training will take time but will help you to hear what you may not have been aware of before and, in time, will help you to help others when you teach. See Section 5.

Try to find your best yellow tone on other head joints, if possible. Some head joints lend themselves more to a range of colours and some have a built-in harshness or loudness, probably because flute players are more likely to buy them! Keep in mind that you are hearing the flute in your right ear from a distance of less than 6 inches away. What the listener perceives from some distance away may be quite different. Your tone needs to be acceptable — and employable. It is a sensible idea to record yourself close up with one microphone and, simultaneously, another microphone at a distance of several yards. Then, compare the two.

The two tones, yellow and purple, should then be transferred to the second octave, which is easier to write about than to achieve. This is because we raise the air stream to go into the second octave, a beginner's habit, to make playing these notes easier, but which now needs some modification. As you move into the second octave, only raise the air stream by the *minimal amount necessary* to keep the same colour and pitch as in the low register and to avoid sharpening any note too much.

The same idea applies to the third octave, where sharpness is a common fault. An electronic tuner is fine for checking yourself, but try not to rely on it too much. The ear needs to be trained to recognise the pitch of notes. It should be pointed out that to achieve different colours in the higher octaves is more difficult. *The Pneumo Pro Wind Director* (Blocki Flute Method LLC) is a valuable tool to help those having difficulties with moving their jaw, to change air direction, etc.

To produce the two tone colours suggested might take some time to achieve, but the result is a more interesting and useful performer who, if patient, will find that rewards will follow. Suitable exercises are set out in my *Practice Book One – Tone*.

Finish your daily tone exercises with one of the beautiful melodies you have already played, underlining what has just been learnt.

MELODIES

Flashy finger technique is admirable, but as Theobald Boehm and others have remarked, 'I prefer to be moved rather than astonished'.

A good way to achieve a command of slow tunes is to practise them. Remember that playing rapidly can also be expressive, it just happens at a faster speed! The few pieces here will get you started: Saint-Saëns, "The Swan'; Gaubert's 'Madrigal'; and the folk song 'Home, Sweet Home'.

Most simple melodies follow a pattern of 16 or 32 bars in length, broken into 8-bar segments. Each 8 bars is subdivided into two 2-bar phrases and a 4-bar phrase. Most of the Moyse *24* and *25 Little Melodious Studies* are based on this simple formula, as are almost all Baroque and Classical melodies. Typical examples are shown overleaf.

Excerpt from Verdi: The Force of Destiny
Fig. 2.3

It is easy to lose sight of this simple format for melodies: the first bar
leads to the second; the third bar leads to the fourth; the fifth continues
to the seventh bar, after which the melody diminishes to its resting place.
To control the dynamics, pitch, expression and the *forward direction of
the music* is not easy and should be regularly practised. In the example
below, a crescendo is made during bar 1 into bar 2, with a diminuendo
on the D; the same from bars 3 into 4 and from bars 5–8. This simple
formula is a start, but tone colour and expression also play their roles,
as well as *expressive intonation*, outlined in Section 5.2.

Chopin: Piano Sonata in B♭ minor, Op. 13
Fig. 2.4

In the next example, the melody can be played as two 4-bar phrases
rather than the usual 2+2+4 phrase:

Beethoven: Piano Sonata 'Pathétique', Op. 13
Fig. 2.5

2.4 TECHNICAL PRACTICE

FINGER TECHNIQUE: WEEKS 1 AND 2; 3 AND 4; 5 AND 6

Acquiring a good technique is far easier when the muscles of the body are still developing. This was made clear to the author after giving a newly-written and difficult finger exercise to about 20 music college students, including a few 16-year-old players, several 18-year-olds, first-year college students and a few postgraduate students of about 24 years of age. After six months of practising them, the younger players were technically far ahead and playing with accuracy, and at *double the speed* of the postgraduates. The significance of this is that we must try to acquire a sound technique when young; don't spend too much time on those enticing solos. The exercise used was from *Practice Book Six*, part of which is shown later, at Fig. 2.8.

The fingers have two sets of muscles to activate them: the *extensors* and the *flexors*. One muscle straightens and the other bends each finger. Both sets are independent and require exercise, and therefore regular practice. Scales and arpeggios are valuable because they reflect the patterns found in almost all music, but specific exercises written to strengthen and speed up the movement of each finger will also be useful to you.

Our plan will consist of a six-week rotating series of finger exercises using three books, each with different note patterns. Though the three books are different, they work very well together as their aim is the same: to strengthen and emphasise independence of fingers.

The three books are:

- Marcel Moyse, *Technical Mastery for the Virtuoso Flutist*.
- Trevor Wye, *Practice Book Six: Advanced Practice*.
- Marcel Moyse, *Daily Exercises (480 Exercises)*.

One book should be practised daily for 25–30 minutes for two weeks; then changed to the next book. You should notice a dramatic improvement in your technique within a short time. The first example is from a Moyse book, shown below.

Weeks 1 & 2: Marcel Moyse, *Technical Mastery for the Virtuoso Flutist*. This sounds daunting, but if the advice here is followed, results will soon be noticed. The example below is in Moyse's handwriting. You should repeat each bar four times.

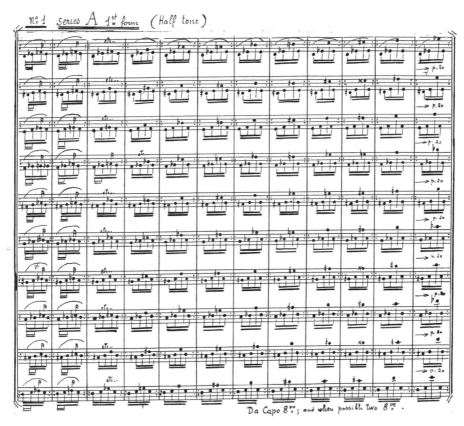

Moyse Exercise (page 7)
Fig. 2.6

Notice that the last line begins on B. Please continue for one more line, starting on C, so that C♯ is the second note.

Continue in the same way on the next page.

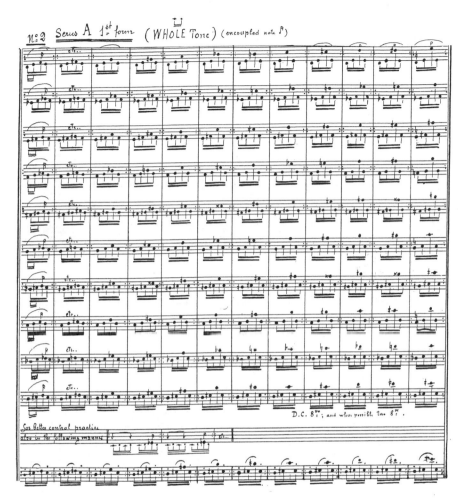

Moyse Exercise (page 8)
Fig. 2.7

To gain maximum benefit, the normal fingering must be used in each bar; be sure to use the little finger for E natural and *do not* use 'easy' fingerings such as the middle finger for F♯ as it will not give the best sound. Similarly, use the first finger for B♭ until it is played alongside F♯, then use the thumb. Why? Because these are exercises *to develop your muscles*. If you prefer the easy option, don't bother to practise.

The third page is not shown, but the starting note is D and the second note is F, so this page is based on minor thirds.

You will need a total of six pages — the sixth being intervals of augmented fifths. It is suggested that for the first few weeks, the first four pages will be enough. Only later should you add pages five and six.

Weeks 3 & 4: Trevor Wye, *Practice Book Six*, page 12, *Advanced Daily Exercises*. As before, use the most difficult fingering. The exercises labelled A, B, C and D are enough for a 25-minute session, though you may go over this time limit for the first two weeks. Only section A is shown below.

Repeat each bar above with the following accidentals using the correct fingering:
(i) as written (ii) with D♯ (iii) F♯ (iv) F♯ + D♯ (v) E♭ (vi) E♭ + F♯ (vii) F♯, D♯ + E♯ (viii) E♯ + F♯
(ix) E♯ + F× (x) E♭ + F♭

Fig. 2.8

Before continuing to the final two-week session of the six weeks, it would be better to establish a routine and familiarity with these first two books for two or three months before moving on to the third book. This is to establish a good practice routine first, and to make some advances with finger independence.

Weeks 5 & 6: Marcel Moyse, *Daily Exercises (480 Exercises)*. Follow the plan set out in the chart at the beginning of the book. It will take a little working out, but it will help you to understand what to do each day.

In the case of a reader who feels that they are behind technically and would like to make a more rapid improvement, they may practise two different books each day — one in the morning and one in the evening, keeping the two practice sessions *as far apart as possible*. Practise the Moyse *Technical Mastery,* and later *Practice Book Six*. The reason for the space between practice sessions is that these exercises are tough on the finger muscles, and even though you may practise other things, an eight-hour break allows your hands to relax and will avoid any trouble with strain.

When practising *all three books*, it is essential to be aware that you are practising rhythmically and evenly. If the result is uneven, you are *practising* unevenness — or, put another way, you are *practising failure*! Regular use of a metronome will help to establish regularity and precision. Remember, it is not just the notes *on* the beats which have to be accurate, but the notes *in between* the beats too.

SCALES AND ARPEGGIOS

Some years ago, I spent a week cataloguing the music for flute and keyboard in London's British Library. A list was made of the music for 1 or 2 flutes and keyboard, written before the year 1800. After a week, I reached the letter E and collected around 1,700 opus numbers, totalling about 7,000 pieces. So, how many pieces are there for flute and keyboard in the British Library *and* all the other European Libraries? Perhaps in excess of 60,000? What is the main compositional characteristic that links these pieces together?…

They are all constructed of scales and arpeggios!

Think about that. It's a good plan, therefore, to practise scales regularly — in doing so, you are mastering the notes of 60,000 pieces! Isn't that more sensible than practising a concerto which may be technically out of your grasp?

The famous English player, Geoffrey Gilbert (1914–1989) was at breakfast one morning, while teaching at a summer camp, when a fellow tutor commented that he had heard Mr Gilbert practising his scales earlier that morning. Gilbert put down his knife and fork and replied:

'There are certain daily activities that one does which includes shaving, showering and other ablutions. These activities also include the daily practice of scales and arpeggios. It is not a matter for public discussion!'

The practising of scales, arpeggios and related patterns should become a daily habit — something to make our playing more enjoyable to listen to, and to make you more employable! Practising scales over one or two octaves is just not practical; our repertoire is written over three octaves, and that is just how scales should be played. A daily scheme for scales can be found in the *Complete Daily Exercises*, where each scale starts on the tonic, ascends to the highest note possible, and then descends to the lowest note possible (C_1 or B_1), finally returning to the tonic. The highest note available to you may be B_4, C_4, $C\sharp_4$ or D_4, but start with what is comfortable, and step by step introduce the higher notes.

For motivation, you could try writing the name of each scale and arpeggio on a slip of paper and putting them into a box. Take one out at a time and play it. If you play it badly, put it back into the box. If it was satisfactory, then leave it out. That way, you will more frequently practise those scales which you can't play.

PRACTISING THE THIRD AND FOURTH OCTAVES

When you are ready to extend your practice into the third octave, it is best done at the end of a practice session, as it can be tiring for the lips. Start by using third octave notes in scales and arpeggios, extending the range upwards to use the notes C_4, $C\sharp_4$ and D_4 as part of your daily practice. Then, begin playing arpeggios from low C for three octaves, adding $E\flat_4$, E_4, and F_4 in subsequent weeks. Even after a short period, you may be surprised at how much easier those high notes become. In time, your lips will get stronger and you will find it easier to form and maintain the shape required for these notes.

STUDIES

The composers of studies (or etudes) generally focus on problems such as expression, articulation, finger technique, embouchure flexibility, a difficult key or perhaps a melodic or musical problem. It is an added bonus when a study has good melodic content. But why bother with studies? Why not just practise pieces? These questions are easily answered: repertoire pieces were written for enjoyment and as an expression of emotion or the love of music. Using them to practise and correct a beginner's faults has a negative impact on the performer, as they will later remember a piece as being formerly used to correct a bad habit. This makes it much harder to enjoy music-making at a higher level. For the younger and less experienced player, this may not be easy to understand.

There are numerous books of studies of varying difficulty by Andersen, Kummer, Briccialdi, Demersemann, Garibaldi, Furstenau, Donjon, Berbiguier and others. One of the most delightful and intelligent books of etudes are the *24 Studies, Op. 15* by Joachim Andersen. The Marcel Moyse *24* and *25 Little Melodious Studies* are also excellent, as they provide good material for overcoming simple musical and technical problems. They were originally written for the Paris Conservatoire students when Marcel Moyse deputised for Philippe Gaubert in the 1920s. Some studies were written as daily exercises, for example the Soussmann *24 Daily Exercises*, most of which are very fine, though not all equally useful. The compilation book *Complete Daily Exercises* contains the most popular and long-standing daily exercises by a variety of well-known composers. A good place to start is with the Reichert 'Study No. 2'; a simple sequence of arpeggios.

ADDING LYRICS

When practising a melody, try adding your own words to the melodic line as it may help to understand stress and release in phrasing.

Andersen: Op. 15, No. 3
Fig. 2.9

This well-known Andersen 'Study No. 3' is a good example. The melody can be better understood by singing 'I love you, really love you, yes I love you' etc. to the melody notes, the notes which begin each slur. Be sure to accent 'love' and not 'you'!

Eighteenth-century music was all about the creation of stress and release in both melody and harmony. One way this was achieved was by the use of the appoggiatura, a beautiful gesture, sometimes called a musical caress, which still often occurs in the music of today. There is more about this in Section 3.4, *The Appoggiatura*. The extract below from Reichert's *Seven Daily Exercises* (available in my book, *Complete Daily Exercises*) is a good way to begin to understand this important feature. The fifth note, F♯ is, in effect, an appoggiatura which is resolves on the sixth note with a diminuendo, and similarly, the thirteenth note resolves to the fourteenth. They are appoggiaturas because they employ a dissonant note not found in the tonic chord of C and requires resolution.

Reichert: 'Study No. 4' from 7 Daily Exercises
Fig. 2.10

Exaggerate this embellishment while being careful of your intonation on the release of the appoggiatura. It is better to start off with an easier key, such as F major (Fig. 2.11).

Adapted from Reichert: 'Study No. 4' from 7 Daily Exercises
Fig. 2.11

As well as the books mentioned previously, a recommended list of studies should include:

The *26 Studies,* found in the Altés *Méthode de flute, Volume 2*. These were written originally as duets, for the teacher to accompany the students, but are also published as a solo line. The original version with the harmony makes the studies far more meaningful and musical.

The *25 Celebrated Studies* by Louis Drouet are pleasantly melodic and encourage an understanding of phrasing and form.

Andersen's *24 Studies,* Opus 30, 31, 41 and 63, the latter containing several excellent studies. You can find free versions of these online, however, it is prudent to look for a reliable printed edition from your local music store.

Jean-Michel Damase's *25 Studies* are of moderate difficulty and his *24 Studies* are tricky, but perfect for bridging the gap between 19th-century and contemporary studies. There are a further six books of Damase's *Studies* in ascending order of difficulty.

Ernesto Koehler's Opus 33 and *30 Virtuoso Studies* (Opus 75) also have their enthusiasts too.

Paganini's *24 Caprices.* There is a choice of transcriptions of these studies and they frequently appear on competition lists.

Leonardo de Lorenzo's *9 Great Studies*. Some of these are excellent for stamina and technique. They are long and difficult.

Holcombe's *24 Jazz Studies for Flute*. These are excellent for encouraging a relaxed approach to music-making and, curiously, even help towards a better understanding of the rhythms and music of the 18th Century. There are two books: *Moderate* and *Advanced*, both help towards removing stiffness in phrasing.

The works of Ian Clarke, Robert Dick and Mike Mower are also most useful for opening the door to contemporary music.

2.5 ARTICULATION PRACTICE

PRACTICE STRATEGY

Generally, articulation offers meaning and musical understanding using punctuation — slurring and tonguing. When we play short notes, or staccato, the length of the notes is determined according to both the dictates of the music and other players involved, as well as the acoustics of the room. It is important to realise that a slur accentuates the first note; two notes slurred together emphasises the first and diminishes the importance of the second. Because the slur has this effect, we should 'go with the flow' and realise that a slur is also a diminuendo — except sometimes! Sometimes? This is a basic principle which can be broken as often as the music demands it. A composer may write a long slur over many notes to indicate a phrase — smoothness, but not necessarily a slur as we would understand it.

Aim to develop a very efficient and speedy single-tonguing technique. There's a tendency for young players to learn to double tongue too soon before a solid single-tonguing technique is in place. Double tonguing should be used only for playing a passage which is much too fast for single tonguing. Remember that oboe and clarinet players only use their forms of double tonguing in special circumstances. It is far better for the purposes of practising to use single tonguing exclusively for a time, as set out below.

SINGLE TONGUING

To obtain a competent and speedy single-tonguing technique it is best to practice without using the tongue at all, using only the abdominal muscles, as in laughing. Notes are made with the breath, so we begin with some easy scales starting each note *without* the tongue. As with most articulation work, several short daily sessions of a few minutes will produce results far quicker than a prolonged exercise session. Start off with the 'Daily Exercise No. 2' from Reichert's 7 Daily Exercises in the *Complete Daily Exercises for the Flute* (Novello), as shown in Fig. 2.12.

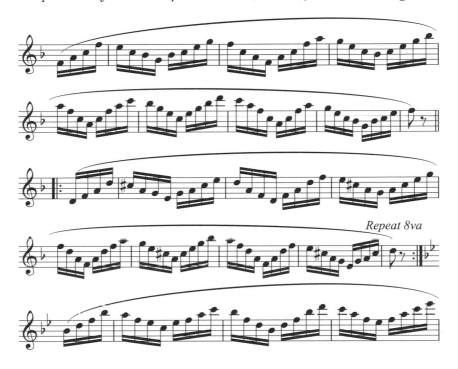

Excerpt from Reichert: Complete Daily Exercises for the Flute
Fig. 2.12

Firstly, play it through with slurs, and then repeat it without using your tongue, playing every note as short as you can. Then practise each key sequence both loud *and* short and after some days, loud and short *and* fast. Doing this will improve your control of the abdominal muscles, and this will pay dividends in the future both for articulation and for flexibility with leaps and octaves.

After articulating without the tongue for several days, for half of your time, switch to adding the tongue, alternating between the two ways: *with* and *without* the tongue.

Expect to spend many short daily practice sessions over several weeks to achieve a satisfactory result. You are training your tongue muscle, and this will take time. Be patient!

DOUBLE AND TRIPLE TONGUING

Be sure your control and ability in single tonguing is first-rate before starting out with double tonguing. This is because much of the action of 'double' and 'triple' rely on an outstanding single-tonguing technique. Keep the tip of the tongue forward, both in single and double tonguing. This will ensure clarity and will later help attain a good speed. Remember, several short daily sessions are more effective than one long one. Try short bursts of fast, almost *too* fast, double tonguing which pushes your speed to its maximum. This will give some hard work for the tongue muscle. If your tongue gets tired, practise flutter tonguing (see Fig. 2.13) a few seconds without the flute as this may help to relax your tongue.

When your semiquaver (16th note) single tonguing has reached a crotchet (quarter note) = 112, it is a good time to begin double and triple tonguing. There are useful exercises set out in the author's *Practice Book Three: Articulation* (Novello), but No. 9 of the Andersen *24 Studies, Op. 15* is also helpful. Practise the single-tongued version as you did with Reichert, then move on to 9b for double tonguing. Don't practise this slowly but rather as fast as you can, in short bursts, i.e. just the first five notes; then the first nine notes at speed. After practising this method for a couple of lines, move on to 13 notes. Continue until you are able to play two or three lines continuously in this way.

Andersen: Study No. 9b
Fig. 2.13

The 'back stroke' ('ke') of double tonguing is generally weaker than the 'front stroke' ('te'). You may notice this in double tonguing if you record yourself. The best method to strengthen and equalise them is to start off the passage with 'ke'. It feels awkward, but at least try to practise several lines in this way. To maintain evenness, reverse the syllables — 'ke-te ke-te' — using the tonguing exercises in the second half of Marcel Moyse's *25 Little Melodious Studies* (UMP), such as No. 18 (second variation) and No. 20 (second and third variations). These are a mental challenge. He wrote the studies changing the usual pattern of four notes of the same pitch to altering just the first in a four-group pattern — and our brain protests.

Next, take away only the first note of the Andersen Study 9b and practise the first half-dozen lines again in this way as shown below. It will help to make the tongue action and finger co-ordination easier in time.

Andersen Tonguing Study, a variation to 9b
Fig. 2.14

Early-music performers use syllables as starting sounds for articulation, as was common in the 18th and 19th Centuries, such as 'te', 'tu', 'du', 'gu', 'ri', and 'did'll'. The phrase 'to tootle on the flute' came from a 19th-century practice of articulating using 'tootle-tootle' to double tongue.

A long-term strategy to obtain the quickest result involves the use of (in effect) two music stands: on one are your usual studies, exercises and pieces, and on the other are the various articulation exercises. This is so that you can rapidly switch from one stand to the other during practice, saving time without interrupting the flow of practising. The switch-over takes place several times each hour for a few minutes only.

FLUTTER TONGUING

This technique involves a rapid flutter of the front of the tongue, usually illustrated by 'frrrrrr'. It is known as an *alveolar trill*. This can be learned by most people, though some (due to a condition called *ankyloglossia*) will find it all but impossible. Another form of flutter tonguing, for those with alveolar problems, is a *uvular trill*. This is made in the throat and produces a growling effect, often used by jazz musicians. The alveolar trill is preferred as it does not create the extra sound which the uvular does. If you have difficulty, start blowing and then try lifting the tongue and think of using 'hhrrr'. The air passing through the mouth should cause the tongue to flutter. Practise a little and often each day to become familiar with this technique.

Try playing a slow chromatic scale down to low C, keeping the lips as still as possible. Contemporary composers write for flutter tonguing to be used throughout the compass — the lowest notes are the most difficult.

2.6 A GUIDE TO FASTER PROGRESS

FINGERING

There are easy or alternate fingerings widely used to help get out of trouble in a difficult solo or orchestral passage, but in exercises and studies we should use *only* the regular fingering, which may well be more difficult. If you are looking for the 'easiest way', as mentioned before, then don't bother practising. Watch out for the following bad habits:

- Using the middle finger for F$\sharp$.

- Failing to open the E$\flat$ key (pinkie) for E$_2$ or F$_2$.

- Holding the left-hand first finger down for D$_2$ and E$\flat_2$, even momentarily.

- Sliding the thumb swiftly from the B$\flat$ thumb key to the B key in sharper keys such as B major.

- Using a variety of shortcuts in third octave fingerings.

In pieces and orchestral passages, we should of course play the passage in the most fluent and smooth way, but only after first trying regular fingerings which usually produce the clearest and the best tone. *You may not notice* — but your audition panel will.

RECORDING

A recording or (better still) a video will help underline both weaknesses and strengths. Do this prior to a performance as you will gain an idea of how others hear you. For example, some players move around a lot, which can be unhelpful, especially if auditioning as a second flute! The principal player will be distracted by someone sitting next to them and writhing about. A video will reveal this.

PRACTISE WHAT YOU CAN'T PLAY

Avoid mindless repetition. Just repeating the same passage over and over may help, but it is not an efficient way to reach a result. That said, a difficult few notes in a finger exercise can be repeated over and over to make the muscles work efficiently. Don't waste time on inefficient practising! Work on weaknesses rather than what you can already do well. Flutists are beginning at a younger age and, together with better teacher training and more reliable flutes, this has lead to students attaining a higher level earlier and an increase in competition for work.

If you find technical problems in repertoire solos, find out exactly what the difficulty is. Perhaps it is a finger problem, such as the movement of the fingers from one note to another, or a series of awkwardly-fingered notes. Work out which fingers are hampering the flow of the passage and find a finger exercise which will help to fix it — or make up your own! If the problem is one of tone or flexibility of the lips, there are exercises which can help to remedy these, including exercises for large intervals, harmonics and bending notes. There are suggestions and sample timetables for practice strategies in *Looking at More Efficient Practice* (Falls House Press, USA, 2009).

MARKING THE MUSIC

Use a pencil to record decisions on breathing, fingering and phrasing. In your future practice, it is unlikely you will change your mind about the interpretation, and so your previously marked judgements will be there waiting to be used again. Use horizontal arrows to denote the direction of a phrase so that it is easily read in performance. Some players use coloured pencils and copious markings. This is a question of choice. Ultimately, it is the performance which matters.

POSTURE

A sensible 'correct' posture has been set out in the *Beginner's Book for the Flute: Part One*, but we've included a useful reminder here. This will also help with teaching too.

The reader may be surprised to find a reference to posture in a book of 'secrets', but it is surprising how many mature players suffer from posture problems, only just seeking help in their later life when the habit has already been well established and harder to modify.

Posture and breathing are the main reasons for standing. Progress is quicker — and practice more effective — while standing. Of course there are instances when you'll be sitting (in an orchestra, for example), but the benefits of good breathing and posture when standing will likely be remembered and applied.

Stand in front of a music stand, with your body and head *both* facing the stand. Turn your head to the left, looking over your left shoulder. Pick up your flute and, without altering the head/body relationship, turn your body to the right so that your head is facing the music stand.

We have a natural inclination to face the person we are talking to with both our bodies and head, but in flute playing, this rule is broken. We must get accustomed to turning our bodies away to the right while the head is looking over the left shoulder. The photo below shows how this looks.

Notice, too, that the left elbow is down and not in the band marching position with the music on the left wrist!

Players commonly use the tip of the thumb to operate the thumb key, but a look at how the thumb moves will show that its movement doesn't need this. It will be more comfortable — in time — to use the part of the thumb shown below. This allows the flute to be better supported.

We often start playing when young, when the flute seems a very long stretch for the right arm and hand. Various designs of flute and head joints have addressed this problem because a good hand position becomes vital for future development of a good technique, especially for the lower notes. A good example is shown below. Ask for advice from your teacher if you are having problems with the position of your right hand.

The right thumb should fall naturally under the first finger. Some people have a longer-than-usual thumb — the thumb will need to be placed further back in order for the fingers to be in a good position on the open cups. There are commercial clip-ons which help to position the thumb more naturally. Otherwise, a piece of cork can be shaped and affixed under the flute body to allow the thumb to be placed further back.

USING A MIRROR

A mirror is an indispensable tool in observing yourself and correcting any peculiarities, including any recurring bad habits. Embouchure and jaw problems can sometimes be better observed and analysed with the aid of a mirror. For articulation, a mirror is essential to observe any movement in the throat, lips, hands, arms or flute, which may be hampering clarity. Posture can also be checked.

THE METRONOME

Rhythm is the lifeblood of music, so your best friend is the metronome. Whether it is to check the overall tempo of a piece or the consistency of the speed of a movement, a metronome is essential. From day to day, we can change the tempo according to mood, health or technical progress without realising it. That said, *it is not a good custom to play with a metronome all of the time*. Rhythm comes from within us and we need to rely on our own rhythmic sense as well as observing and listening to others in ensemble playing. Use it to check tempos before that all-important audition.

A few rules:

- A piece or etude cannot be considered prepared until it has been checked with a metronome for consistency of tempo and rhythm.

- Don't even think of a concert performance of a work with piano or orchestra before checking it for consistency of speed.

- It is surprising how there may be small changes in tempo in different sections of a work.

The prime consideration in any orchestral audition is rhythm. To test out an orchestral passage, practise with different speeds, checking yourself with the metronome. This will help you to be more flexible and confident with any special requests or deviations which may be asked of you.

IMPROVISATION

In Baroque times, improvisation was an important part of musical study. In fact, much 17th- and 18th-century music relied on the performer using some improvisatory skill in their interpretation. It was common to embellish within the repeated section of a sonata, but to what degree was dependent upon the tempo and style of the piece as well as the country of origin. Justify your repeats by saying it a little differently the second time.

In past times, unless the player was very talented and experienced, they usually prepared some embellishment to some degree, though the result was still intended to sound spontaneous. A little improvisation once or twice a week will soon help to develop ideas on decorating a phrase. The book *Looking at More Efficient Practice* contains a CD with recordings of 72 bass lines, about 50 of which have been used since the 14th century. They can be transferred to a portable listening device for convenience.

MEMORY

The quality of performance is our primary aim. If this is achieved by playing from memory then do so; if a performance is better by reading from the music then this is the way for you.

Memorising ability can be improved by training. Some have difficulties playing from memory — perhaps it is the fear of making a mistake that gets in the way. I once asked the legendary violinist Yehudi Menuhin if he ever had memory lapses in performance. He replied:

> *'The only time I ever forget a passage*
> *is when I am trying to remember it.'*

Whether or not you decide to perform from memory, it is a good plan to regularly take your eyes off the page you are practising and rely on your memory. This is good preparation for orchestral playing, where awareness of the conductor and other players is an essential skill.

VIBRATO

This is a frequently discussed topic amongst flute players, perhaps because both its usage and method of production have been controversial. Some have said that vibrato should not be taught as it is 'something you *feel*'. However, string players are taught exactly how to create vibrato — and so should flutists. Some teachers just allow it to happen with their students but this might have long-lasting, unfortunate results as they may develop a throaty wobble which may be almost impossible to eradicate or modify. Quite commonly, a dysfunctional vibrato has been learned without the help of a teacher. Examples are *chevrotement* (Fr. 'quivering', and often referred to as goat-like), or a vibrato of the wrong amplitude or speed. Some players develop a vibrato using the jaw or lips. Any deviation from an even vibrato *within the tone* is very difficult to correct. Put simply, vibrato should help in the performer's efforts to present the music expressively and not hinder it.

Vibrato is a part of a performer's box of expressive tools and should be an ingredient of the tone and not something added on top. Violinists suggest that it should be *inside* the tone, and the player shouldn't cause it to tremor in such a way as to confuse the ear and the pitch of the note. To accomplish this takes practice and effort.

If your vibrato is defective in some way, then the best and direct way to fixing it is to start with long, straight tones. I have seen many efforts on the part of teachers to help the student by modifying the existing vibrato, but it rarely seems to succeed. Perhaps this is because, however it is learned, it quickly becomes part of the musical character of the player, almost part of their personality. The surest way of correcting it requires much patience and starting again from the beginning. It means a week or two of vibrato-less playing, a period which may test your patience, but has to be done.

After a couple of weeks of this and without playing any pieces, begin by training the abdominal muscles to give regular pulses rather like laughing or coughing. This pulsation should then be practised until smooth. The pulses over several days should be increased so that about four pulses per second is achieved. Only when this has been completed might the throat muscles take over. It sounds simple but it will take time and patience. The details are fully set out in *Practice Book Four: Intonation and Vibrato* (Novello). This approach seems to work quite well, though it is a long haul.

Vibrato enhances and gives life to the tone, though some Baroque players may dispute this, maintaining that musical expression does not always require vibrato. For most current orchestral or recital players, the tone will need this addition.

FLEXIBILITY

The ability to be able to acquire flexibility in both the lips and jaw when moving around the three octaves is an important skill in solo and orchestral playing. In the past few years, flute soloists, looking for new repertoire, have exploited this effect by transcribing violin solos. A violinist uses wide intervals to give harmonic support to the melodic line by outlining the bass line and revealing the harmony. The flute is also good at this compared to the other woodwind instruments, but it will take slow practice to begin with, working to ensure each note is played with a good tone and intonation. It soon becomes apparent that every note has its own particular lip and jaw position as well as air speed and air direction. Attention to this detail is necessary for a good tone and intonation, but ways must also be found to minimise the movements involved, with the aim of speeding up the notes and maintaining the connection between them. Suitable material for this can be found in the studies of Soussmann (No. 19, a shortened version of which is also quoted in *Practice Book One*), Marcel Moyse's *24* and *25 Little Melodious Studies*, and Andersen's *24 Studies, Op. 15*.

2.7 FLUTE LITERATURE

FLUTE REPERTOIRE

A comprehensive list of flute repertoire can easily be found online. It is wise to keep up with what is new, including newly-arranged pieces, and to do this you can join an internet flute discussion list. New pieces and commissions by flutists are notified on these lists and often linked to performances. Keep up with what is new!

Flute conventions are also a must. Performers are laying themselves on the line to perform to an audience of flutists — pieces which they may have commissioned or arranged, and must justify by their performance. Publishers also have booths to present new publications; they may also offer discounts. Some publishers have an email list to notify players of newly-published works for the flute.

ORCHESTRAL REPERTOIRE

There are many books containing the best known solos, but knowing the accompanying orchestral part is essential to understanding how to play it effectively at auditions. For the most popular audition pieces, at least a sketch or indication of the accompanying orchestral part is a *must* in the publication. It is impossible to fully understand a solo without reference to the orchestral part accompanying it. For further reference, a miniature score is a great help.

I asked two well-known orchestral principals about their orchestral life, and both said:

> *'As soon as the orchestral schedule is posted,*
> *I head for the library to get the full score.'*

There are specialist books too which feature the Bach Oratorios and Cantatas and more modern orchestral works.

PICCOLO REPERTOIRE

There aren't many piccolo study books; specialists often use the popular flute studies such as the Andersen *Op. 15*. After all, the piccolo is a higher-pitched flute and, as such, needs to be treated melodically.

Dedicated studies including orchestral repertoire are listed in the Bibliography at the end of this book.

In the 19th Century, piccolo repertoire was performed almost exclusively for amusement with titles usually about birds. Many such solos have been reprinted in the past few years, both in albums and as solo pieces, and are quite difficult to play well. Included in the repertoire are piccolo duets either with orchestra or piano accompaniment.

2.8 SPECIAL AND SENSITIVE FINGERINGS

INTRODUCTION

As orchestral players will know, there are many easy or alternative fingerings for particular passages just to make the solo smoother or to satisfy the demands of a particular conductor. These are kept at the ready, and are used promptly when the situation demands it. Some players have a large repertoire of these special fingerings and others players simply practise the problem passage using the regular fingerings, perhaps preferring the challenge of simplicity. Alternative fingerings can be used to adjust the pitch where intonation is a problem, and are also useful where extreme dynamics are required, or to prevent a note from 'cracking'.

There are many special fingerings; however, only the ones most used by professional players are presented here — these are the most popular.

If a special fingering is required, the internet will usually provide answers — or you might try any of these excellent sources:
- Walfrid Kujala's exercise book *Vade Mecum* (Progress Press)
- Larry Krantz's website
- *Special Fingerings for Advanced Flutists* by Ervin Monroe (Little Piper)

LOW REGISTER

The resonance and tone of the left-hand low register notes A, B♭, B, C and C♯ can all be improved a little depending on the flute used and whether it has a B foot. The extra length of the foot can help some notes, but the shorter C foot can also help others. The only way of knowing is to try them — some flutes respond to these fingerings better than others.

A₁: To play this loudly and resonantly, add the G♯ key, right-hand first finger and the low C₁ key — this will allow you to push into this note. It is useful when it is the final note of a piece or when extra strength is required.

A♯₁: Add low C♯ and/or low C and B keys for added resonance.

B: Add the right-hand third finger for added resonance. Also try adding the low C♯ key too.

C₂: For extra resonance, add either the right-hand second and third fingers plus the low C♯, or the low C, or the B. Try combinations of these to help you.

C♯₂: It is usually sufficient to add the right-hand second and third fingers to help it to resonate, but each flute is a little different. It is best to try various combinations of these together with the low C♯ or low C keys. Often, this fingering does not improve the note by itself but allows the player to 'dig in' to it more, which may improve its resonance and help stabilise its pitch.

SECOND OCTAVE

E♭₂: When playing a long *pianissimo* note it can be difficult to stop it going flat. The right-hand second finger can be rolled to the left toward the first trill key to depress it *a little* — just enough to allow this note to sound clear and with less air. This has become so useful that some players bend the trill-key touchpiece sideways towards that finger to make it easier, especially if the player's fingers are small or narrow. An example of its use is in the second movement of C.P.E. Bach's E♭ Sonata, as shown already on page 45 (sometimes attributed to J.S. Bach). A repairperson can easily help modify this for you, if needed.

E₂: You can prevent 'cracking' and make it clearer by adding the second (lower) of the two trill keys already mentioned in Section 1.5, *Altering the trill key*. Take care as it can sound peculiar unless used with caution, and generally only when playing quietly.

F2: When playing *pianissimo*, add the second trill key as for the E♭2 above. Also, as above, take care.

A2: Add the G♯ key when playing quietly. Adding this key slightly sharpens the A and helps to avoid turning the flute in. It can be added to B♭ but is less effective.

B♭: When playing *pianissimo*, finger E♭2 and remove the left-hand second finger. This is a sharp note and will need flattening. Useful as the final '*pp*' of a piece.

C3: When playing *pianissimo*, finger F but remove the right-hand thumb. It is sharp and will need flattening.

THIRD OCTAVE

C♯3: Play as for C♯1 but take off the left-hand first finger as an alternative C♯.

D3: When playing quietly, add the right-hand third finger and first trill key. This will sharpen this often-flat note.

E♭3: To help flatten, lean on the first trill key for '*ppp*' which will sharpen it (see E♭2 above). Also, try using the low C♯ key and the D♯ key *at the same time*.

E3: To flatten this sharp note, leave off the right-hand little finger. If this is not enough, add the ring (on an open hole flute) of only the right-hand third-finger key, without covering the centre hole. The first trill key can be added, though take care as it will also make this note even sharper than it already is!

F3: When playing quietly ('*pp*' and '*ppp*'), add the low C♯ key. Some players use this as the standard fingering when playing slowly, preferring its pitch and quality. When playing loudly, add the right-hand third finger.

F♯3: Use the right-hand middle finger and the low C♯ key.

G3: To flatten, finger low D, add the D♯ key and remove the left-hand thumb.

A♭3: Add the right-hand second and third fingers and D♯ key. This is often known as the 'long' A♭. Many players use this as standard, as it is flatter.

A3: Add the low C♯ key when playing quietly.

B♭3: When playing *pianissimo*, use the left-hand first and third fingers, place the thumb on the B♭ lever, then add the right-hand first finger on the first trill key plus third finger. This is known as the 'Mignon Fingering' from the flute cadenza in Ambroise Thomas's *Overture, Mignon* which ends on a pianissimo B♭3.

B3: Add second trill key (use both) and add right-hand third finger. The D♯ key is optional.

C4: With the left hand, use the first, second and third fingers (no thumb), and with the right hand, use the first finger and half-hole left-hand second (with an open hole flute) or leave off. As an option, add the low B key. With fast scales, play top B and remove the thumb when ascending to C3 and replace it on descending.

2.9 TRILLS

LOW REGISTER

Low C♯/D♯ trill: This is rarely seen, but has arisen in opera. When the player is solo and seated then a strip of material such as a bandage can be wound around the right leg above the knee; stuck to this, between the knees, a small pad or cork. When the passage arrives, the player places the C♯1 *key cup* on the pad and then trills the D♯ key. The alternative is to place an elastic band around the C♯1 key, trilling the D♯ key as before. In other situations, the C♯1 key can be held shut by an elastic (rubber) band — remove immediately to prevent tarnishing of silver or gold flutes — or, as in the case of a piece where the first player has a left-hand trill, the two players switch parts: the second player plays the left-hand trill whilst holding down the low C♯ key with their free hand of the principal player.

Low C and C♯ trill: A similar tactic to the above.

SECOND OCTAVE

E♭2/F2 trill: Always start with the normal fingering for a note or two so that the ear hears good-pitched notes before using only the middle finger.

F♯/G trill: Playing F♯1 or F♯2 requires an extra key to be lowered — the right-hand third finger. For brilliance and purity, and where time allows, a better trill is made by shifting the first finger up to the left of R1, to trill the *real* F♯ key. Some players use this for lyrical passages where a more beautiful F♯ trill is required and where time allows.

A♭/B♭ trill: It is best to start with all three fingers trilling, quickly reducing to two fingers and ending with just the middle finger. If carefully practised, it makes for a better trill than simply trilling with the left-hand middle finger, which results in the upper note being dull and flat.

B/C♯ trill: You may need a custom-built B/C♯ trill key. Trilling with both finger and thumb will give a more brilliant trill with better intonation. An example is in Nielson's *Concerto*.

B/D *tremolo*: As in the Berkeley *Sonatine*, the two trill keys can be used to play D (provided it is practised), aiming to stop the D from being too sharp. If it is too high, just for this piece, a small piece of *plasticine* or *playdough* can be added underneath the trill-key touchpieces to prevent them from going down too far. This could also be stuck to the cork.

THIRD OCTAVE

E3/F♯3 trill: This is common, such as in the Mozart concertos and at the end of the first section of the Fauré's *Fantasie*. Using the thumb is fine in a quiet trill but this sounds worse when playing loudly. Try trilling A and B whilst holding down the *second* right-hand trill key. This gives a brilliant *forte* trill, needed for these pieces. It is less easy to get to the next note but this can be remedied with practice.

G3/A3 trill: Use the left-hand first, second and third fingers as well as the thumb, and with the right hand only the E♭ key; start with the thumb off and trill using the left-hand third finger. Also try fingering G3 and alternately trilling the first trill key and the left-hand C♯2 key. This is good for a short trill, and with a little practice it can be extended for longer trills, if necessary.

3

Section 3
Professional Strategies

Introduction

Several well-known players over the years have commented, usually for humorous effect, that getting a job is largely personality plus a little talent. If you take a handful of professional players and ask them the best way to get a job, you will get a variety of opinions. One principal said that the second flute's most important job is to be first in the coffee line. Others might insist that musical success requires days, months and years of endless practice and preparation. These statements are exaggerations, but with a tiny bit of truth in them, as we shall see.

3.1 PERFORMING

PERFORMING WITH THE PIANO

A work for flute and piano requires the players to maintain eye contact where possible. Take careful note of performers who play well in front of and with their backs to the pianist. Observe a string quartet: does the leader play in front of the other three players? Of course not, but some flute players stand in front of the pianist and are even obliged to turn around to indicate to them to begin. This is an arrogant approach.

In a competition, a contestant may walk onto the stage to perform using the music stand positioned by the previous player. Be wary of this. Move the stand to wherever it is most convenient for you.

Ideally, the piano should be positioned so that the keyboard itself is within sight of the audience — slightly angled with the tail end moved back, away from the audience. This allows the flutist to use the curved section of the piano to play from, maintaining eye contact with the pianist and still having a connection with the audience. There is no rule which says the piano must be placed on stage exactly side-on to the audience.

The angle of the lid depends on the piano, the pianist, the tonal power and projection of the flutist, the stage *and* the room's acoustics. The best position is one which gives the best balance. Some nine-foot grand pianos can be quite strong, even when the pianist tries not to overpower the flutist. One solution is to adjust the lid, which (on most pianos) can be opened fully or partly, or be completely shut. When the lid is fully open, the player can angle the flute to use the piano lid cavity, playing with the end of the flute into the lid. This reflecting feature of both the open lid and the soundboard will help to project the sound. The piano lid is to keep the dust out — not to keep the notes in. Players regularly performing with a piano might make their own 'half-way' stick. A handicraft store will sell hardwood dowels which if cut to around 18–25 inches long and covered in black tape, will allow a better piano tone than the integral short stick and will weigh almost nothing for travel purposes.

When playing with a harpsichord, note that the lid is either fully open or removed altogether. Never play with the lid closed.

The stage floor itself can behave like a drum skin and boost the lowest notes of the piano, which may become overpowering. A piece of matting or carpet placed under the piano will help to alleviate this problem.

It can be hard to judge both the performer's tonal projection and the hall's acoustics from the stage, so it's often helpful to have a sound check with a friend or teacher. Try the different registers, dynamic extremities and articulated passages, and ask your friend to comment.

In a hall with a 'proscenium arch' across the stage front, take care to play in front of this if possible; if you cannot, try to be as near the front of the stage as you can. Usually, such an architectural feature might dampen your projection, making your job harder.

THE PIANIST

There is a current fashion in some countries to refer to the pianist as a 'collaborative pianist'. This is nonsense. Let us hope the pianist will always be 'collaborative' and helpful; as will the flutist. This name has come about in the past few years from the pianist's role being credited as an 'accompanist', an 'assistant' or even 'assisted by'. I have seen posters where the pianist's name was printed in smaller letters than the soloist, and so this repercussion is understandable. At times, the pianist will be playing more prominently than the 'soloist', and for some passages entirely on their own. Some assistant! The two players, flutist and pianist, are duo partners; both should be advertised equally and, more importantly, treated equally.

During performance, avoid turning to the pianist without good reason. This may be misconstrued and distracting — the pianist may expect that something is required from them. Also, the tone of the flute is emitted in equal parts from three places: the end of the flute, from the keywork (directly outwards) and also from the player's embouchure. Turning to face the pianist changes the sound received by the audience.

Similarly, avoid conducting the pianist. You can indicate your start with a gentle nod, but avoid excessive movement.

THE PIANO PART

The intelligent performer will be familiar with the piano part of the piece. The pianist isn't there simply to follow but to take an active duo role, therefore make a habit of *always* practising from the piano score, even if you are not a pianist. The general shapes and movement of the piano part will help to give you a better idea of what is going on and the interaction of the parts. Make a note of any comments by the pianist in your flute part. The flute copy should be treated just as a guide during performance.

TUNING CAREFULLY

You have all seen the flutist who pecks a couple of notes and then nods to the pianist to begin. It seems common these days for the flute player to be sharp — some very sharp. This comes about because of a failure of several factors. To tune carefully the soloist must first play the tuning note with a good tone, usually A2, as if it were a note from the piece. Secondly, since A2 is not the best guide to the overall tuning of our instrument, it is more constructive to play A1, and then D2 followed by A2 (see Section 5.2 regarding D2 problems). D2 is useful because it uses the full length of the flute and is a better guide to the right-hand notes; though A1 may be in tune, its octave (A2) may be sharp. If these three notes are used in tuning up when practising, you will become familiar with this procedure and perhaps improve your intonation. Do not begin to play the music until you are satisfied with the tuning and don't be embarrassed if this takes a little time. It would be far more embarrassing to hear a playback recording with bad intonation.

PLAYING IN TUNE

Careful checks with a tuning device during your practice will indicate if there is a problem with intonation. Most often, flutists become sharper during the performance as the flute gets hotter — and the player too. This will show up during practice. Stage lights will also contribute to this. Be prepared to pull out the head a little during the performance. Placing yourself within the curve of the piano will help you to hear any differences.

MARKING BREATHING SPOTS

The carefully marked breathing spots put in during practice are often impractical during the excitement and stress of a performance. During practice and rehearsal, allow extra breathing places, perhaps closer together, to allow for the excitement of the occasion and the resulting tendency for you to have less air.

CHOREOGRAPHY

Excessive movement can be distracting and even appear silly. Just once, have someone take a video of you when performing and then play it back at double speed. This should cure you of any excessive or repeated movement. There is no need to remain motionless, but any movement should be part of the emotional impact of the music on the performer. This is too often copied from someone else — perhaps the performer's teacher. On many occasions, performers have been observed waving the flute around and even deliberately stepping forwards, backwards or sideways, presumably attempting to make a greater impact on the performance. This is idiotic. One wonders what they would do when making a recording? Remember why the piano, the stool, the music stand and often the performer's dress are all coloured black: *it is to take away the attention from both the stage and performers, and to help the audience concentrate on the music.*

MAKING ANNOUNCEMENTS

There are a few simple ground rules about speaking from the stage. The first is to never turn your head away from the audience while speaking. This can have the effect of rendering part of your announcement inaudible. Remember to keep facing the audience whilst speaking and do not turn to the pianist, a common mistake.

Another simple rule is to speak slowly — slower than you might normally do — so that those at the back of the hall have an equal chance of understanding what is being said. A trick used by trainee actors is firstly to aim your voice at the gallery (if there is one); in other words, aim your voice high. The second is to lower your overall voice pitch, something which might be practised. It only requires lowering a little to be more effective.

Thirdly, always check the pronunciation of composers' names carefully. For example — 'Doo-tee-yer' (Dutilleux) not 'Doot-ty-low'. There is a full list of common flute composers and an easy-to-understand pronunciation guide in the back of *Proper Flute Playing* (Novello, 2000).

BOWING

Do not bow before the audience has applauded. Wait for a second or two; you are *responding* to their applause. Always bow at the same time as your pianist — *never* bow alone, with the suggestion that the pianist played no part in your success. It looks arrogant and unprofessional. Perhaps, prior to your concert, agree and plan with the pianist how you might bow together.

3.2 HELPING YOUR CAREER

ETIQUETTE

Getting work in the profession can be very competitive. To stand the best chance of getting a job you should act and behave in a professional manner. Make eye contact when speaking with people.

- Remember good social manners, for example, cover your mouth when yawning or coughing.

- Always shake hands firmly. Avoid the limp, wet-fish approach.

- You cannot thank people enough for something they have done for you. Better still, thank them by letter or card, even for small acts of help or advice which they may have given to you. If you are unsure, reverse the roles: what is your feeling when you are thanked for helping someone? Thank them. Do not hesitate.

- Be respectful and take care not to say anything to which the most sensitive person could take offence.

- Use good formal grammar when addressing an audience or at an audition interview. Ask yourself: 'How do I want others to think of me?'

- Ask a friend to choose your publicity photo. It is quite common to make a poor choice. Look at the photos in a flute society magazine, often chosen by the soloists themselves. It is surprising how some photos are ill-chosen, so ask for advice. The photo chosen by a friend may not be your choice, but you should trust them.

- Avoid exaggerating when you write your CV. If you haven't done very much, then write less. Avoid listing too many teachers; it begs the question, 'why did you need so many?'. Don't write nonsense or waffle. An experienced interviewer will be able to tell if you are as experienced as you say you are.

- Be properly prepared for lessons. Follow the advice offered; if you don't agree with the teacher's suggestions, try them anyway. Trust your teacher — or go to another.

- Listen to other players and other students — there is always something to be learnt. The experience of attending live concerts will add to your knowledge and skills. Attending flute conventions is a must too, as there is opportunity to hear new compositions or newly-revived pieces. There are always new sounds to be discovered. The trade stands are a good place to look at new ideas, new flutes, newly-designed head joints and generally to be up-to-date on what is fresh. It is also very useful in meeting other players who may be helpful in your career.

- Be considerate of your fellow students — they may be your colleagues one day.

- Always be early: cultivate a reputation for being reliable and punctual.

- Respond to all correspondence promptly and with good grammar.

- Return borrowed items when you said you would, and within a reasonable amount of time. For many years, I used a rubber stamp on all my music, which read: *This music must be stolen as I never lend music*. It did remind people to return music.

- Always carry a piccolo in your bag on a professional date.

- Try to do one thing each day to further your career, however small. This does not include practising because you always do that.

- Join your national and local flute societies. You will always learn from the experience of attending conventions or by reading the society newsletters. Better still, as your career progresses, become active in its organisation. If you get involved, it is an easy way to meet people who may help you.

- Remember that the flute community is relatively small. Word gets around. Teachers and players talk to each other, perhaps about you. Be remembered fondly.

- Go backstage afterwards following a recital. This is your first port of call to thank, congratulate or even commiserate with the performer. You will be remembered in a kindly way for doing so.

- Finally, develop good taste — 'Le Bon Gôut', as it was known as in the 18th Century — in at least some of the following: music, appearance and dress, conversation, correspondence, social manners and good dining behaviour.

LEARNING NEW WORKS

Learning a new piece from time to time should be a part of your practice schedule. The extremes of musical history are the most ignored: the late-17th and early-18th Centuries, and contemporary music. A newly-composed work often creates a dilemma if there is no existing recording to listen to first — it can be disheartening to spend time learning a difficult piece if it turns out not to be worth the trouble. Nowadays with the internet and video media it's much easier to find existing recordings of relatively new works. That said, when learning a new standard repertoire piece, avoid the temptation of listening to a recording for hints on interpretation until you have developed your own ideas about this. It is harder to learn a piece well if another player's performance becomes the basis of your own interpretation. The printed music usually provides all the information necessary to arrive at a reasonable understanding for performance. For some compositions, though, it is more difficult to imagine how the piece goes; perhaps a single listening should provide sufficient clues. Only after learning a piece might other player's interpretations prove useful. This will help you to acquire *Good Taste*.

Light music and jazz are useful in developing a sense of phrasing and learning to loosen-up any stiffness in playing. Curiously, jazz also helps in lightening up 18th-century music too, especially 'inegale' and other techniques. The *24 Intermediate Jazz Studies* and the *24 Advanced Jazz Studies* by Bill Holcombe (Musicians Publications, USA) are a good starting point, and are accompanied by audio backing tracks.

Soloists are hard pressed now to find *really meaningful* new pieces, particularly when performing at flute festivals and conventions. Although there are many thousands of pieces for flute and piano, few are really worth playing. As festivals and conventions have become more common-place, soloists try hard to find little-known works and introduce them to the public. This is easier than it sounds as there is usually a very good reason why a piece has been neglected and rarely played, though from time to time little-known gems are discovered around the world. Some soloists transcribe works originally for other instruments and play them on the flute.

ORCHESTRAL AUDITIONS

Be properly prepared and really *know* the orchestral score into which the solo fits. Be prepared to play very softly and really loudly when the music — or the orchestral panel — demand it. *Always* check the excerpt with a metronome early on in your practice and again well before the audition day.

A good audition strategy is to reverse the roles — imagine putting yourself in the place of a member of the auditioning panel. Firstly, think about what it must be like to listen to a wide variety of players. What do you think are the common mistakes made by candidates? Make a list of the problems you think you might hear. What is the number one priority? *Rhythm!* The most common errors are typically non-rhythmic playing, poor intonation and inattention to small details such as dynamic markings and phrasing.

Consider this scenario: you are Candidate Number 37 on the second day of auditions. While you are waiting outside, you can hear the player before you, playing wonderfully through the closed doors. Do remember that everyone *sounds better through closed doors*. Don't let that put you off. The panel have heard 36 players already. What are the common mistakes or faults? Here are some tips to help you stand out from the crowd and avoid the common mistakes:

- Take care with pitch when playing quietly — many will play flat.

- Ensure you hold trills for their full length and play them tidily. Don't allow the difficulty of the trill to govern your speed. Practice the trills from D_2 to E_4 and from G to A as well as some of the trills in the third octave. A weak technique, or uneven fingers, highlight these problems.

- Observe the full length of notes, especially tied notes, and *do not cut them short*. An example — the 3/8 melody which the flute and cor anglais play just before the virtuoso section of Rossini's *William Tell Overture*. The trill is also often cut short.

- Ensure you are familiar with the accompanying orchestral part.

- Do not play passages too fast, such as in Mendelssohn's 'Scherzo'. Consider why this solo was chosen; the audition panel are not checking whether you *have* the tools, but how you *use* them.

- Avoid copying an interpretation you have heard on a favourite orchestral recording. This might inadvertently lead to exaggerating and distorting the rhythms and phrasing.

- In a concerto, write your own cadenza if you can.

- The famous *Daphnis et Chloé* solo: in the opening scale, just think about the E♯3 and aim for that note on the way up the scale. It will help you to play a smooth scale — as it has helped others.

- Learn an emotive solo such as in *Daphnis et Chloé* with a metronome first. Understand the rhythms well before 'interpreting' the piece.

- Practice the piccolo just in case it should be asked for.

There are many alternative 'easy fingerings' to help you (see Section 2.8). The whole idea at the audition is to perform well, whatever the fingerings. Only the flute player on the panel will be aware of what you are doing and will be on your side. The rest of the panel probably have no idea and wouldn't care anyway. It's the performance which matters, not how 'correctly' you use the beginner's fingering chart.

BE PROPERLY PREPARED

Remember to check the solos with a full score, and keep the orchestral accompaniment in your head as you practice the solos. It may seem surprising but, as mentioned previously, it is quite easy to spot an experienced player from one who is unaware of the greater context.

Prepare to play the solos of Bach and Brahms in a different style. For example, in more recent times, players are sometimes asked to play without vibrato. Practise this. Examples are in the solos of Bach's *Passion According to St Matthew* and *B Minor Mass*.

Commonly, the orchestra hires a competent pianist for the auditions. If you are using the audition pianist it is advisable to avoid music with an overly-difficult piano part, or music which requires ensemble preparation or problems with which the pianist may not be familiar. Also, carefully mark the piano score in red to make your intentions clear to the audition pianist. This will save time and explanation during your short rehearsal — if there is one! Finally, again, the number one priority is rhythm; check all your solos with a metronome.

3.3 COMPETITIONS

To be successful in a competition is partly a technical skill. The choice of pieces and how they are played — the interpretation — is also a competition technique. The wise competitor obtains advice on how to show their best side and not their failings. It is surprising how some players choose a piece which shows weaknesses in articulation or weakness of the low register. The interpretation of the works, particularly of the Bach family and of Mozart, should be aimed at the widest public or the majority of the jurors so as to gather as many of their votes as possible. Listening to recordings by jury members may help. A historically-authentic performance may be 'correct' (and it may please your teacher) but could annoy some of the jury. One jury member remarked: 'I hate it when a player tries to educate me.' The whole idea of competing is to *win* — not necessarily to be right.

Competitions are international, national and local, but the basics are the same. International competitions attract players from all over the world and so the jury members are also chosen worldwide, which can result in a wide diversity of opinion. For most competitions, there is usually a preliminary round via submitted recordings. Preparation for this is as important as the live rounds. Never send off a poorly-recorded submission. Be sure that the music is recorded in a quiet studio with good equipment, otherwise the poor quality may irritate or distract the judges. I have heard audition submissions with dogs barking — an interesting addition, not called for in the score!

With regard to microphone placing, a very experienced recording engineer once told me, 'The best results are usually from a microphone placed six feet high and six feet away from the performer'. Be aware that any further away will make a nice echo but make it almost impossible for an adjudicator to come to a decision.

In big competitions, there may be four rounds for which the music needs to be learnt well beforehand. There have been occasions where a candidate, not realising they might pass through to the next round, failed to properly learn the pieces for the later rounds.

For such a mixed jury, the performances should be in a way which appeals to the widest possible range of listeners. A cranky interpretation is not a good idea, though displaying imagination and creativity *is* a very good idea. I can remember one candidate who had practised imitating the traverso in a Baroque piece, which sounded awful — a ghastly mistake!

Some competitions require several pieces to be played from memory. This can't be picked up in a just few practice sessions — it can take a while. You might find it helpful to try a few performances as a test. It is important to know the accompaniment as part of the memory test. The piece must be wonderfully performed, as well as being performed without using the score.

International competitions usually follow the rules laid down by the World Federation of International Music Competitions. Jury members vote a mark for each candidate out of 25. For the first round, the cut-off point is 18; for the final round, it is 21 or 22 (any lower and the performer is unsuccessful). The single highest and lowest scores by jury members are deleted from the total to avoid any extreme voting. Sometimes, the average marks, except for the first round, are added together to the final round marks to give an average. This ensures that competitors must consistently do well in each round, covering the various styles requested by the panel. Jury members are not allowed to vote for their own students or for students well known to them, or who have attended a masterclass with them within the past three years.

As a jury member sitting for many hours, it is fascinating to hear how each competitor tries to impress both the audience and the jury with their stage mannerisms, their interpretation and their performance. Some try everything from facial expression, walking about the stage whilst playing, exaggerated body movement, curious interpretation and even elaborate dress.

The jury is made up of players of wide experience, usually from different countries, each of whom may have different performance tastes as well as their own opinion about what makes the perfect finalist. Some attach great importance to a clean performance with no mistakes. Some members will study the score looking for mistakes. However, when a really captivating player is on stage, juries often write nothing — they sit back grateful for the chance to listen to a gifted musician.

What can the performer do to prepare properly? The obvious underlying technique is to play the flute well. This is the foundation. The performer is asking the jury to test them, and so, as a start, the four basics should be well understood: tone, technique, articulation and intonation. These are just the tools. After this comes the interpretation and character of the music, and the personality of the player. To gain the most number of points, the performance should be something close to what most of the jury expect. As mentioned before, if a performer's interpretation is rather personal or even eccentric (in an effort to impress), they may end up with a bad reaction from the jury. The player may even be right, but scores no marks. Nevertheless, the player who uses their imagination also scores marks.

Performers should practise at the pitch specified in the competition information sent to them. The standard pitch varies in European countries and around the world from 440Hz to 446Hz. Ensure you practise at the given pitch.

For some players, memorising may be a new technique. A performance can be better when memorised, but usually only once the player has lost the fear of forgetting. As mentioned before, one might need to perform at some public concerts to gain confidence and experience.

Some players have no idea how to play loudly or softly whilst remaining in tune; perhaps they can play in tune when playing softly but become very sharp when loud. A player who frequently practises like this might not be aware of the transgression, but the jury will notice and they will not enjoy it.

The use of body movement is becoming less popular now in some countries. Most sensible players today realise that it doesn't achieve anything except to make the soloist appear rather silly. Remember the concept of a black piano, black stool and a black music stand...?

My advice for those who have failed to advance to the next round — *stay and listen* to the remaining rounds. This is by far the most valuable part of the competition. They can imagine themselves as a jury member and try to find out why others were selected while they were not. It is also valuable for the performers to approach the jury members to ask for feedback on what they can do to improve their chances for the future. Usually, the reason a player doesn't get through to the next round is simply that the other players are better. Jury members will often try to help and encourage without giving too much criticism.

It is important to remember that each of the entrants is most likely the best player in their university, school, city or country — but there are many universities, schools, cities and countries…

3.4 PERFORMANCE PRACTICE — AN INTRODUCTION

It is all too easy to think in chunks of history such as 'Baroque', 'Classical', '19th Century', 'bravura', 'Impressionist' and 'modern', but remember that music gradually evolved over time. We might forget that the 17th- and 18th-century musicians hardly travelled as we do, and so changes of style or fashion were slow to move around. We must try not to put music into labelled boxes.

The notes which follow about Baroque music are more detailed than later periods because this was a time of great change, both in our instrument and in the style of composition and performance; most importantly, this music was very influential on later music.

3.5 PERFORMANCE PRACTICE — BAROQUE MUSIC

BAROQUE MUSIC

The term 'Baroque' refers to music written between around 1580, through mid-Baroque in about 1630 and late-Baroque around 1730. The term was not commonly used until the 19th Century, where its meaning is *strange, bizarre* or something *unusual* in music, art, architecture, etc. Some contemporary music is like this, so could be referred to as Baroque! When spoken, the word is 'ba-rock', not 'ba-roke' — or worse, 'broke'!

The next sections are concerned with performing the flute music of the period which sets down principles or rules, most of which apply to later periods too.

THE BAROQUE FLUTE

The flute used during this era is conically bored with a cylindrical head, usually made of boxwood, or other woods and even of ivory. The flute has one key for D♯, but could have two — the extra one for E♭. It has three or four joints (head, middle, lower and foot joints), though some better-quality flutes were made with *corps de réchange* — a set of alternate extra middle and lower joints used for performing at different pitches. During the 17th and 18th Centuries, the performing pitch varied between countries with no common agreement. Strangely, this is still the case today, though the differences are now much smaller. Travelling performers were obliged to carry flutes of different pitches and/or *corps de réchange* in order to cope with the pitching standards found in different cities. The pitch of A around Europe was variously from 386Hz (roughly G natural in modern terms) to 415Hz (G♯), up to 430Hz, and all the pitches in between. Later still, it rose to the 460s. For the performer, it required an embouchure of great flexibility — and a number of extra joints or flutes!

PERFORMING STYLE

Baroque music is largely about the principle of conflict — the creation of *tension* and its *release*. This 'tension and release' is found in the harmony of the music and by the use of the appoggiatura — the 'most important ornament in 18th-century music' (C.P.E. Bach: *Essay on the True Art of Playing Keyboard Instruments*, 1753).

Many of the signs and symbols written before 1800 require interpretation but were clear to the 18th-century performer as a common agreement between composer and player. The composers were often performers in their own right, so this gave insight into common performing practice.

After about 1800, the signs generally needed little interpretation; players performed the music according to how it was written.

Much of Baroque performing practice was based on the harpsichord, the king of instruments, and what it was able to do. Since harpsichords were incapable of playing loudly and softly, ornaments were used to help highlight notes and place accents, or to draw the listener's attention to a particular phrase.

The so-called 'rules' of this music were not invented for us to follow; they were written down as a record of current 18th-century performing practice. Modern performers may find that instead of having to learn a new language, the rules may only be reinforcing what they already know or instinctively feel. When the modern performer is familiar with them, they will find that much of it is simply common sense. Later music also owes much to the earlier Baroque style, though its development was in line with the change in architecture, dress and language — less fussy.

OBBLIGATO OR CONTINUO?

An obbligato part is one which must be played as it is written in order to realise the effect of the whole composition. It does not mean *ad libitum*. In effect, a sonata with obbligato keyboard is a trio (in three parts): the keyboard's left-hand part, the right-hand part and the flute part, together forming three independent solo voices in balance. On the other hand, in a work for continuo, the solo part is the solo melodic line, the bass supporting this with the figures under the bass line indicating the harmony which can be filled out by the keyboard player, perhaps decorating it according to personal impulse and the requirements of the music. These two distinctions are an important influence on the performance.

BAROQUE TRILLS

These usually, but not always, start from the upper note. This is dependent on several factors, well beyond the scope of this book, but its purpose was to create tension and release as in an *appoggiatura* (see the Bibliography for suggestions for further reading). Trills are there both to decorate the musical line and to create an elegant exit in the cadence to a phrase. Starting on the upper note creates a dissonant appoggiatura — tension, followed by release.

The trill mirrors Baroque courtesy — when a gentleman wished to leave the presence of a lady he would *make a leg* by placing his left leg forward as a prelude to a bow. As he bowed, he might say 'Madame, I am your most humble and obedient servant', and then (depending on the social status of the lady) he might walk backwards three paces before turning his back on her. The trill, therefore, is an elegant exit to a phrase.

Should you consider beginning with the upper note, lower note or not at all? This is not as important as the *way* in which the trill is played. It is an expressive device, and not necessarily to be played quickly. In a slow movement, a slower, expressive trill is preferable as it is unlikely to disturb the character of the music. Trills should be rhythmic too. A trill can be compared to a blending of two colours. Imagine a spinning disc with alternating colours — the colours blend seamlessly and without preference of one colour over another. Similarly, trills should equally sound *both* notes, without bias.

TEMPO

An approximate common pulse throughout a sonata is something to aim for and may help in deciding a 'good tempo' for the individual movements throughout the work. Let us consider the J.S. Bach's *Sonata in E Minor* as an example. The crotchet (quarter-note) pulse in the first movement might match up to the minim (half-note) pulse of the second movement and also match the crotchet note value of the third. In the fourth movement, the crotchet can match the minim. In this way, there is an affinity between the movements, just as there is in the various dishes comprising a good dinner. To keep an *exact* relationship is not the idea, but the movements are brought together by this affiliation.

THE LENGTH OF SOUND

The sounds made by a harpsichord and an oboe, for example, can differ in length. Sometimes, a note played by a loud instrument — or one with a sustained sound — should be played shorter to leave room to hear the accompanying passage. Explore tiny silences in performance; silences can help emphasise, accent or draw attention to a part of a phrase or a note. They are a part of the language of music. Small silences are important before strong notes where they can help to highlight the down beat or the first beat of a bar. An experienced actor will know all about silences.

BARLINES AND BEATS

The barline denotes the presence of the beats, which can have a profound effect on the feel of the music. The first beat of the bar is the strongest, but there are of course exceptions — for example, when the composer writes accents on other beats. Harmonic considerations are important too, and a dissonance is usually accented even when it is on the weak beat of the bar.

ARTICULATION

Articulation is the language of music. With speech, if we say a person is inarticulate, we are suggesting that they are unable to sufficiently explain or describe. On the flute, we think of articulation as tonguing, but it is the variety of tonguing which gives a phrase meaning. A common expression was that we 'tootle on the flute' which, as mentioned before, comes from the 18th and early-19th Centuries when 'tootle-tootle' was a method of articulating pairs of notes. The basics of this were set out before in Section 2.4.

The use of slurring, tonguing and staccato help to convey the meaning of a phrase. A slur over two notes emphasises the first whilst diminishing the importance of the second. The player can make this more obvious by making a diminuendo during the slur. One approach is to treat short slurs as diminuendos. In the case of a pair of notes, even if the player tries to play them with the same emphasis, the use of the tongue on the first note naturally gives it prominence. As C.P.E. Bach writes, an appoggiatura is always slurred to its resolution, which is played softer. This is just a general guide to this important subject: more detailed information can be found in the books mentioned in the Bibliography, and further guidance regarding articulation practice can be found in Section Two. Some players say that a slur is a diminuendo — *except sometimes!*

THE APPOGGIATURA

In French: *port de voix*, from the Italian *appoggiare* ('to lean upon'). Some think of the appoggiatura as a musical caress in which there must be a release, or it is not a caress! An appoggiatura, usually a dissonance, is always slurred to its resolution with a diminuendo to the second note.

> *'The appoggiatura is the most important ornament in our music: it creates tension and release.'* — C.P.E. Bach

> *'C.P.E. Bach is the best teacher we have ever had — and anyone who doesn't believe that is a ****!'* — Mozart

RHYTHM IN BAROQUE MUSIC

In Italian music, everything is usually carefully notated. In French music, a series of notes of the same value in an *allegro* dance movement are sometimes played unequally (*inégale*); the correct rhythm is open to interpretation. *Inégale* is employed much like the swing of jazz. Degrees of *inégale* can vary, but simply 'jazzing it up' won't do. The amount of *inégale* should be practised in the following way:

- Draw an imaginary line on the floor. This line represents an even, equal rhythm.

- Three further lines (steps forward) can be imagined:
  ○ the second is *slightly* uneven
  ○ the third is triplets
  ○ the fourth line is dotted notes.

- You can use the exercises on the next page to practise the rhythms, but any ascending and descending scale will do.

- Start by evenly playing the exercises, as written. Next, play with the imagined 'fourth line' — dotted rhythms. Then, the third line, in triplets, and finally the second line.

Inégale is roughly the second line you have drawn on the floor, which is a little uneven, perhaps jazzy, but not triplets. It doesn't matter if you play this exercise in a rather jazzy style to begin with. You can decide later what you consider to be in *Good Taste*.

This exercise should result in an ability to control the amount of *inégale* according to the passage and the style of the piece. *Inégale* can also be considered as a dynamic imbalance between pairs of notes too — something to think about.

Next is the *Bourrée Anglaise* from Handel's *Sonata for Flute in G*. As the title is in French, we might assume it is to be played in the French style — with *inégale*. Notice that there is only one visible slur in the whole movement. Other than specifying *legato*, this slur also indicates that the next phrase is to played with even notes. Then return to *inégale* again at bar 15.

A famous French vocal group* was said to have wanted to sing Classical music *inégale*. The way they found to do this was by singing a series of even notes with the syllables; da-ba-da-ba-da. The rhythmic effect produced was slightly unequal because 'da' is direct and the 'ba' very slightly late, giving the unequal effect.

*The Swing Sisters

Handel: 'Bourée Anglaise' from Sonata for Flute in G
Fig. 3.1

DOTTED NOTES

'The first note should be longer, the second shorter — the exact proportion to be determined by the character of the music. The reverse rhythm is the reverse rule.' — C.P.E. Bach

This suggests that dotted rhythms should be exaggerated when playing, i.e. lengthen the dotted note and shorten its complement. This is *not* a rule set in stone; the exact rhythm is determined by the character of the music.

Dotted notes
Fig. 3.3

In the example above, the note on the first beat can be played slightly longer and the notes on the other beats played with the correct rhythm.

VIBRATO

Vibrato was not a special topic for discussion in the 18th Century because it was only occasionally used as an ornament. Nowadays, it is a major source of interest and study amongst young flutists. If the reader were to listen to good period players they would soon realise that there isn't any vibrato as we know it; more importantly, it seems unnecessary. The music simply does not require an incessant wobble because there are more subtle means of expression, such as dynamics, colour and phrasing. Perhaps this is hard to grasp for a player nurtured on wall-to-wall vibrato. Some players believe that the tone of the Baroque flute doesn't lend itself to vibrato, which does little to enhance the sound.

To achieve a better understanding, listen to the 'king' of 18th-century instruments, the harpsichord. It was the foundation stone of ensembles and orchestras, and its character widely influenced performance on other instruments, including the flute. The harpsichord can't employ vibrato, and (as you learned earlier) there are no loud/soft options — so how does the harpsichord player communicate expression? They achieve it through the subtle adjustment of note lengths, timing and rhythm. Modern made harpsichords often have pedals and the means to rapidly change tone colours through use of the pedals, however this may not be in *Good Taste* because pedals were not available to 17th- and 18th-century players but rather a modern addition.

EMBELLISHMENT AND ORNAMENTATION

Embellishment is the art of adding notes to decorate, colour and add emphasis to a melodic line. A thorough look at this topic is out of the scope of this book, but one important point should be mentioned: you should first obtain a clean and unedited copy of a score, which is known as an *urtext* or facsimile edition. You shouldn't embellish what may already have been embroidered by an editor. Also, take care before you begin — to pepper a decent tune with poorly-considered ornamentation is to ruin it. Handel is a case in point; his sonatas have good tunes and are largely best left alone, although they can still, with care, be decorated. The modern performer, unaware of *Good Taste,* may simply add mordents and nothing else. This is like adding tomato kotchup to everything.

There are two mordents shown below. The second mordent (with the line through the symbol) is a rapid three-note alternation between the written note and the one below, and known as an *inverted mordent.* Sometimes, a player may decide go downwards twice, just to make it more brilliant — a sort of double mordent of five notes. Another player might add a note before the mordent, either starting with an upper note or a lower note. The first example below (without the line through it) is not a mordent at all but a short *trill,* perhaps of three or five notes, sometimes more. This ornament is often indicated using a simple cross above the note.

Mordents   **Played**

Ornaments
Fig. 3.4

The cross symbol (in the third given example) indicates an invitation to do *something* — perhaps a trill, mordent or turn — to decorate the note. Even when a composer writes '*tr.*' above a short note, they are leaving the choice of ornamentation open to the performer.

Ornamentation varied in different countries, with composers each having their own conventions and preferences. Some composers did not indicate trills, especially at cadences, as they would assume that the performer would know where and how to decorate the notes. Perhaps they thought it seemed pedantic to write down the obvious. The modern player can be forgiven for assuming the absence of written ornamentation (in their reliable urtext copy) as an indication that the composer did not want any. The cadence always requires a trill. Handel, like most of his contemporaries, omitted the trill sign assuming the player understood the 'rules'.

Listen to a selection of first-rate players to gain a better understanding of ornaments and embellishments. The opinions and interpretations are likely to vary.

Part of the magic is to make the ornamentation sound fresh and improvised — as if it has been thought up on the spot. Through multiple performances of the same piece, a performer will find it challenging to maintain the same freshness as when it was first played.

DYNAMICS

Baroque music did not usually indicate dynamics, as the written notes were in fact more of a basis for interpretation. The performer would create the performance from the written 'guide', and so the dynamics were considered part of the performance rather than of the composition. Where dynamics are freely sprinkled throughout the work, it is usually the result of an enthusiastic editor suggesting a suitable way of performing the piece. Some performers write in the part how they would perform it. The most informed performers will choose to obtain a clean and reliable urtext edition and use their own imagination.

MOOD WORDS

An interesting exercise suggested by 18th-century teachers was for the performer to take a phrase of four or eight bars, and then apply some mood words — such as *tenderness, gaiety, flattery, pathos, majesty, resignation, jocularity, boldness*, etc. — and then to illustrate these words in performance. They should sound a little different from each other.

For example, we can start with the word 'melancholy' and list similar words, such as *sad, unhappy, gloomy, depressed, glum*. Next, aim to convey the subtle distinctions between these words in your performance of a particular phrase. Finally, try the reverse — *happy, cheerful, delighted, blissful*, etc. You'll have to work very hard to make these distinctions.

In the Bibliography, there is a list of recommended books to read on style and ornamentation, but if your time is limited you might read only one: *The Interpretation of Music* by Thurston Dart (Dent. 1954). It is slim, easily understood and full of common sense. It will start you off on the right road to both *Good Taste* and a successful and informed performance.

PREPARING A SONATA

Consider the following suggestion: the performance should more importantly reflect the composer's intentions rather than the emotions and feelings of the performer.

Use a 'clean' edition, i.e. one in which the editor has not added their personal ideas on performance. An urtext or facsimile edition will do very well. Avoid being misled by clumsy additions in clumsy editions.

The accompanying instrument, whether harpsichord or piano, should be reflected in the performance of the sonata. The choice of instrument can affect both note lengths and slurs. Remember that the harpsichord is naturally a quiet instrument and unable to express a wide dynamic range. In a large hall, its contribution will be greatly reduced.

The acoustics of the performance hall may influence your choice of style, articulation, and speed. For example, a church can be very resonant; a slower speed will aid with acoustic clarity, and this could be further improved by shortening the notes beyond what is indicated in the score.

First look through the whole piece and decide on its general character — whether each movement is light, heavy, smooth, lyrical, melancholy, vivacious, etc. You should always keep this in mind as you practise and perform the music.

It's important to choose an appropriate speed. How does the bass move? If it is a slow movement in common time, try to feel the movement in 4 or 2 and not in 8 as this may make for a bumpy performance. If it is in 6/8, you should feel the 2 beats per bar rather than 6. As famous violinist Carl Flesch wrote in Part Two of his *Violin Method*:

> '*Barlines are there for the beginner; it is the
> duty of the artist to overcome the barlines.*'

You might be *thinking* of six beats to help you count, but take care that your phrasing doesn't reflect this subdivision.

Remember that time signatures with a similar common pulse — such as 3/2, 3/4 and 3/8 — are different in style: 3/2 is broader and slower than 3/4, with 3/8 faster and 3/16 livelier still.

When practising each movement, mark the principal cadences with a letter, perhaps in red. These will serve as mileposts to help indicate points of arrival and departure — places to 'aim' for in your performance.

Play all repeats and justify the repeat by saying it differently the second time around.

Take the first steps to decide on phrasing and slurring. As you mark in a slur, put that same slur in the parallel phrases *in the rest of the movement*. This makes for consistency of ideas in performance. Don't make too much contrast of articulation (such as between long tongued sections with long slurred sections) unless there is a good reason, otherwise the movement may seem too mixed in its ideas.

Decide on the dynamics regarding the phrasing, then mark these decisions throughout the movement in parallel places, for consistency.

Write out your cadenzas, if there are any, and keep them both short and in the style of the movement. Although a cadenza may be written down by the performer, in the performance it should sound as if it had just been made up. Only an uninformed musician plays cadenzas written by someone else. However short, a cadenza should contain an element of surprise, to delight and enthuse the audience. (See the Bibliography: Mozart.)

Finally, as discussed in Section 3.5, *Tempo*, look for a common bond between the tempos of each movement so that there is some uniformity of ideas, rather like putting together a fine meal.

As mentioned before, try to develop *Good Taste* (known as *Le Bon Goût)* and elegance in how you play. Note that upper-class social thinking through the 18th Century — by those who could afford flutes and the time to play music — was dominated by the search for *Good Taste* in dress, furniture, art, porcelain, silverware, and in fact anything decorative, including music. The acquisition of *Good Taste* was the main aim of a gentleman's education. (At the time, women rarely played a musical instrument and even more rarely in public.)

So, to help develop *Good Taste* why not start off by listening to some of the harpsichord music of Rameau (the *4 Suites* and *Pièces de Clavecin en Concerts*), Couperin's *Ordres* and the short pieces by Duphly and Daquin, who were composers during the reign of the Sun King, Louis XIV of France. This could be described as 'perfumed' music, and it should help acquire a feeling for the period.

PERFORMING BAROQUE MUSIC ON A MODERN FLUTE

Apart from the head joint, our modern flutes are cylindrical, and when compared with Baroque flutes this makes for quite a marked difference in loudness, tone quality and range. The Baroque flute has a small embouchure hole which is hardly covered by the lower lip, unlike the Boehm flute. The tone of the Boehm is broader, 'bigger' and can, according to the player's preference, use more harmonics or colour. It is easier to be agile as it speaks faster; it can leap large intervals easily; it can play articulated extended passages quite loudly, enough to be heard in a large concert hall; its intonation and tone are more even in all keys.

Though not everyone will agree, the two obbligato sonatas of J.S. Bach, the B Minor and the A Major, together with the G Minor and E♭ Major Sonatas of C.P.E. Bach (often attributed to J.S.) sound more balanced in the counterpoint and passage-work if a piano is used because it matches the modern flute so well. The continuo sonatas, E Major and E Minor, sound good on both harpsichord and piano, depending on the characteristics and style of the player, though a modern large-toned flute player can make some harpsichords sound weak, which will ruin the balance of the performance.

It is important to remember that there are several kinds of harpsichords, from a simple continuo Italian single-manual model to a grand double-manual French or German model. A performance will be effected by the choice of instrument. There are modern harpsichords too, which have pedals and stops to vary the colour and loudness.

The harpsichord lid should always be fully open or removed entirely. A good balance between the flute and keyboard should far override the desire for 'authenticity'. Bearing in mind the instruments, the approach to the performance and the creation of tension and release through the harmony or melody, much of the character of the music will derive from the how the ornaments and cadences are played. To ignore this is to anaesthetise the performance. The articulation of the two players, flute and keyboard, should be uniform too: the harpsichord has a clearer, sharper attack and a quicker sound decay than the piano, so the flutist should endeavour to match up to this articulation. The piano can sing and sustain more — this must be considered. The flutist should ask the pianist to play a solo keyboard passage in an obbligato sonata and emulate the note lengths, phrasing and loudness as only through this method will the two players sound as a team. You might ask your pianist to play the first few bars of the first movement of the E♭ Sonata by C.P.E. Bach (attributed to J.S.) and then copy the note lengths in bars 18–19 of the flute part.

The modern flute can slur large intervals, whereas the Baroque flute doesn't usually slur more than a fifth; it is worth considering this when attempting to imitate the Baroque instrument. In the excitement of a fast or elaborate musical section it might be tempting to switch to a 'slur two, tongue two' articulation (for example), but the more intelligent musicians might take a more thoughtful approach.

With all that has been said, the modern player might assume that Baroque music is naught but a set of strict and fussy rules... yet the poet, architect and author Thomas Hardy (1840–1928) wrote:

> *'I knew that too regular a beat was bad art...*
> *in architecture, cunning irregularity is of enormous worth.'*

Further food for thought, from poet Robert Herrick (1591–1674):

DELIGHT IN DISORDER

A sweet disorder in the dress
Kindles in clothes a wantonness:
A lawn about the shoulders thrown
Into fine distraction:
An erring lace which here and there
Enthrals the crimson stomacher:
A cuff neglectful, and thereby
Ribbons to flow confusedly:
A winning wave, deserving note,
In the tempestuous petticoat:
A careless shoe-string, in whose tie
I see a wild civility:
Do more bewitch me than when art
Is too precise in every part.

Lawn: A shawl. Stomacher: a length of material around the woman's middle.
Petticoat: an underskirt.

3.6 PERFORMANCE PRACTICE — CLASSICAL MUSIC

ROCOCO AND CLASSICAL

Before the Classical period there was a transitional development known as *Rococo* — a late-Baroque movement which reacted against over-decoration, symmetry of design and the limitations imposed by the Baroque composers. It has a more playful and witty style, and this can be seen in much of the flute music from C.P.E. Bach and D. Scarlatti, as well as the music of lesser composers such as J.G. Müthel (D Major Sonata is a great example). This ushered in the Classical period (roughly 1750–1825) with contrasting tunes and clearly defined phrases.

It was during this period that the instrumental families of the modern symphony orchestra developed — woodwind, brass, strings and percussion. The instruments also developed and evolved, with added keys, altered mouth holes and variations in bore size, all of which modified the tone, allowing a more brilliant technique and influencing the style of composition.

ARTICULATION AND ORNAMENTATION

The preceding principles were still part of composition and performance; the appoggiatura still created tension and release; trills still decorated cadences. Operatic arias had a lasting effect on the flute music of the time, developing a more vocal style. This affected expression and performance practices, and the use of different forms of articulation was more evident. Vibrato was still largely unnecessary, though Charles Nicholson experimented with it in the 1820s by notating when it was to be used, purely ornamentally. He also employed *glissando* in slow melodies, as did Giovanni Paggi and some others. The conventions regarding articulation, though, were still broadly the same: a slur is almost always a diminuendo.

In the example of ornaments within Mozart's music, notation of appoggiaturas is rarely consistent — as pointed out by Robert Levin — and this can create problems and questions for the performer. Looking at the opening note of the *Andante in C* (for flute and orchestra), Mozart writes '*tr.*' as an indication for an unspecific ornament. What are the options? Here are a few:

Trills
Fig. 3.5

There are several options — perhaps too many. A simple solution, having weighed up all the alternatives, is to choose the one which makes the music sound most beautiful and the one you like best!

Most problems with Mozart arise with the appoggiaturas or grace notes which have different written values. The experts assure us that Mozart was not consistent with the note values he gave to these tiny notes. What do we play? The simple answer, again, is to try as many ways as are possible and to choose one which seems to do the most justice to the music.

All trills begin on the upper note — except sometimes. The exceptions are shown either by the omission of an auxiliary note or by the inclusion of the lower auxiliary. Whether upper or lower, this is always played *on* the beat. The trill begins on the *lower* auxiliary when it is approached from below (often following a scale passage) and to give more finality at the end of a long section, for example in the first movement of Mozart's *G Major Concerto*, bar 89. When the trill is a short one, particularly in the faster movements, it is unimportant whether it starts on the upper or principal note. It is more important that when the trill is short, it either begins on the main note or, if you wish, on a *short upper note*. A common error is to play a shorter trill, for example in the first movement of Mozart's *D Major Concerto* (bars 32, 50, 58, etc.) and the first movement of his *G Major Concerto* (bars 66, 125, etc.). Remember that it is a *dotted* trill.

The Novello edition of the Mozart Concerti contains advice on writing your own cadenzas — very important for personal development and essential if you wish to be competitive.

Mozart is quite clear about whether or not a turn should be played at the end of a trill — where none is written, none should be played. A turn has the effect of giving finality to the phrase, as in a cadence. In many cases, the trill is simply decorative and is not intended to indicate the end of a section.

3.7 NINETEENTH-CENTURY BRAVURA

ENTER THE BOEHM FLUTE

The flute underwent many changes during the early 19th Century. Keys were added, initially to allow for easier and swifter ornaments, but later to include the demands of changes in compositional style requiring a more agile technique and an extended compass. Other woodwind instruments were similarly changing: the clarinet had been invented in Germany around 1699 and the other woodwinds were developing a bigger range, and more key work was added to enable a faster technique. Flute makers were experimenting with bore size and finger hole sizes. By the early 19th Century, the flute had many more keys and was made using materials other than boxwood and ivory.

New compositions abounded, especially for the amateur players, but were mainly operatic potpourris or variations on well-known melodies of the day. The approach to compositional ideas seemed to emphasise charm and vocal elegance, and often included sections of virtuosity to astonish and delight the audience.

Theobald Boehm produced his first flute in 1832 with a cylindrical head, retaining the conical body. His second flute design was introduced in 1847 with a conical head and cylindrical body, almost identical to the flute we all play today.

Composers such as the Doppler Brothers, Eugène Walkiers, Kaspar Kummer, Louis Drouet, Ernesto Kohler, Frederick Kuhlau and Giovanni Paggi took advantage of the greater technical freedom and wider range of dynamics to write pieces which charmed and astonished audiences. These are commonly played by flutists today, but need suitable care in performance so as not to unwittingly reveal technical weaknesses. If the piece seems too difficult, then it *is* too difficult. We still hear performers in an unequal struggle with a difficult piece — something which is best done in private. Better to play an easier piece well.

Later in the 19th Century there were even more developments in flute manufacturing and keywork design, and composers such as Demersseman demanded *fff* or *ppp*. It is not unusual to find a dot above a note indicating brevity – just for that one note. It is easy to ignore these small signs but they do add a special inflection to otherwise run-of-the-mill passages.

ARTICULATION

Preceptors (instruction books) from Jacob Wragg and Charles Nicholson recommend using 'tootle-tootle' for double tonguing and 'tootle-too' for triple, though Nicholson also suggests double tonguing using 'digga-digga', 'tuca-tuca' and 'tittle-tittle' — evidence of the variety of methods aimed at improving technique and speed. There is plenty of further reading around this subject, though it is doubtful that this would greatly benefit the modern performer.

TRILLS

Trills — or 'shakes', as they were usually called — were still illustrated in 19th-century instruction books as being played with the *upper note* first, as an appoggiatura. It later seemed to vary between countries. When the piece is particularly romantic, the trill does sound better when the *lower note* is first held, beginning a little slower before speeding up. It adds excitement and results in a more dramatic close to the phrase.

3.8 CONTEMPORARY MUSIC

MULTIPHONICS

The use of multiphonics is primarily a 20th-century technique, first called for in the solo flute work *Sequenza* by Luciano Berio, though the technique of singing whilst playing has been known since the 18th Century, and was used by Carl Maria von Weber.

The Other Flute by Robert Dick (Mel Bay Publications, Inc. 1989. Second Ed.) is a classic instruction book in this technique, discussing specifics including key clicks, jet whistles, quarter tones, whistle tones, glissandi and many others. There is plenty of information to be found online too. The modern flutist should not bypass acquiring these techniques which are a useful addition to your tool bag. There are several inadvertent advantages too — when you know how to play three notes at the same time it is easier to learn how to avoid doing just that! Many players produce accidental multiphonics ('splitting' or 'cracking' a note), commonly on E_2 and F_2 when moving around in the second octave.

More recent innovations include a quarter-tone flute made by Eva Kingma and a glissando head joint by Robert Dick. There are also many players who experiment with beatboxing. All of these innovations might stimulate composers to write in new styles.

Beatboxing is a form of vocal technique which typically imitates drum beats and percussion, however this has been around in African music since the 19th Century; singers would stamp, make breath and other noises as part of their music.

With the introduction of the many extra techniques expected of a modern performer, players have found that the fourth octave, previously played with some difficulty, is now far easier. Persistent use of these notes makes for easier access, given time and regular practice. It all seems a far cry from Paul Taffanel's view that the notes above high B (B4 on a B foot flute) were not considered as part of the compass of the flute.

'18th-century duets; 19th-century stand; 20th-century players'
John Ward RA

CIRCULAR BREATHING

This is a technique used by flutists (and other wind instrumentalists) to play a continuous tone without interruption. To accomplish this, the air supply is topped up by breathing in through the nose whilst air stored in the cheeks is pushed out through the lips with the tongue. It is an old technique used by glass blowers from the earliest times, and on instruments from around the world.

Some modern works expressly demand this technique, and some players have found the skill useful for performing transcriptions of violin works which would otherwise be impossible. It is an easier technique to acquire when young. More traditional players declare that playing classical works without a breath sounds unnatural. In the earlier days of learning this technique, it was thought easier to achieve with a straw and a glass of water, however it is much quicker to learn it directly using a head joint or the complete flute. Robert Dick and others have written excellent instruction books which make the whole process relatively easier. (*Circular Breathing for the Flutist* by Robert Dick.)

These are just a few of the extended techniques used on the flute. Some teachers teach these to beginners both for fun and to acquaint them with these techniques.

3.9 CAREER STRATEGIES

SETTING UP A WEBSITE

This is the best way to get yourself known — to promote concerts and your recordings as well as your teaching and playing activities.

Aim for simplicity. The first page simply needs to list the contents and a click on any of these should take the visitor through to the page concerned. Avoid asking visitors to register or create an account as this puts folks off. Instead, add a visitor counter to keep track of the traffic to your site.

FINANCE — PAY YOUR BILLS PROMPTLY

Perhaps this is obvious, but some people are slow in paying up for professional services. If you are responsible for paying other performers, pay up yesterday! You will gain a good reputation for reliability by being prompt.

If you are new to professional life, check on paying your taxes. If you are earning, you will have to pay at some point and it is better to be ahead of the game than to turn a blind eye until someone finds out.

If you are self-employed, remember to save your receipts for everything even remotely connected to your career, including clothes, cosmetics and hair appointments, not forgetting the expenses associated with where you teach.

COPYRIGHT AND PHOTOCOPYING
3.10

COPYRIGHT

Copyright laws exist to protect the interests of the owner, and without this protection many composers and publishers would struggle to produce new music. It is a fascinating subject, but copyright can be complex and may vary in different parts of the world. It is therefore important that you are aware of the basics so that you know what you can and can't do when using someone else's work.

In many territories, a piece of music (a 'work') remains in copyright during the lifetime of the writer plus an additional 70 years after their death. In the case of co-written works with multiple contributors, copyright exists for 70 years after the death of the last living writer. Once the copyright has expired, the work enters the 'public domain'.

In addition, any printed scores retain a separate 25-year typographical copyright, after which the edition also enters the public domain. This means that publishers can create their own edition of works that are already in the public domain, therefore creating a new copyright in this edition only, which lasts for 25 years.

So why do we need to know this? How is this relevant to us as musicians?

You will likely want to perform these musical works to a paying audience. You may also want to arrange such musical works, to print the lyrics or extracts of the music in your programme, or to make photocopies for your accompanist. For musical works not in the public domain, you will need to obtain permission from the copyright owner. For any musical works in the public domain — for example, the music of Mozart — you are free to use the music as you please, however if creating a new arrangement or replicating a printed score you will need to ensure you are using an edition which is in the public domain, otherwise obtain permission from the publisher. This permission is often granted in the form of a licence.

PERFORMING COPYRIGHT WORKS

Organising a concert can be a very rewarding experience, however you will need to ensure that you have a performance licence in place. The venue may have such a licence, so it is worth checking this first, but you should be aware that you may need to sort this out for yourself. Various performance collection societies handle the distribution of royalties given to relevant copyright holders. 'PRS For Music' is the royalty collection society for performances taking place in the UK. You can search online for more information on how to obtain a performance licence. A fee is payable to the royalty collection society for the works performed, and a portion of this fee is then distributed to the composer, publisher and/or arranger.

REGISTERING NEW WORKS

If creating your own compositions, you can register with these royalty collection societies to ensure that you receive appropriate royalties from anyone wishing to perform your music in a public concert. New arrangements may also be due such royalties, but take care over various prevailing or existing rights — it may not always be obvious which works are or are not protected by copyright laws, or who controls the rights to a specific work. There are trade bodies and societies set up to assist with these matters, including the Music Publishers Association (MPA).

USING PHOTOCOPIES

Photocopying is so easy, but it can wreck the lives of composers and publishers. How? It's important to first know how print publishing works.

A composer or arranger asks a publisher to publish a piece. When it finally appears in print, they receive nothing until *you*, the performer, buy a copy. Over time, the composer receives a small royalty based on sales. Remember that the publisher is also taking a big chance in publishing a work as they must offer retailers a good discount deal to allow them to make a profit and to cover costs. Some contemporary composers choose to print and sell their own music to maximise the small profit on sales.

When preparing printed scores, the publisher first creates images of the music. *This image is subject to copyright as it is the publisher's work*. Remember that the composition and the printed image are both registered as copyright. To photocopy a piece is *theft*, pure and simple.

Some competitions state rules which prohibit photocopying; candidates can be disqualified for using illegal photocopies.
Can you photocopy for study purposes? Excerpts in academic dissertations will require permission from the publisher, but this is perhaps unnecessary for private study. When in doubt, check with an authorised music publishing association.

I have quite often been invited to sign photocopied editions of my own works. The usual signature I write:

'To Eliza Jones, with love, and thank you for the theft of my music.'

HEALTH ISSUES
3.11

PAIN, TENDONITIS, TENNIS ELBOW, PINKIE PAIN, SHOULDER PROBLEMS AND SORE LIPS OR MOUTH

Pain is commonly a signal to stop what you are doing. It is well beyond the scope of this book to give advice as these problems are usually specific to the person concerned.

Tendonitis is a strain of the arms or hands and is best cured in its early stage by rest. Even if that takes a while, rest is the best cure.

Right-hand pinkie pain often results from a change of hand position, or from an effort to alter its movement by bending or curving it to allow easier movement, or to access the lowest keys. This is fine when the player is young, as the body allows changes without protest. However, making big changes after about the age of twenty should be only be attempted with caution. It is thought that our bodies reach a peak of development during our mid-to-late teens — after this, stiffening occurs.

If the player demands an uncomfortable procedure from their body, it could protest; so, proceed with caution. If such a change has to be undertaken, then practising a little and often is better than sustained practice. If discomfort is experienced, the standard practice is to place the hands or arms in hot water, refreshing the heat every few minutes. Of course, if a painful strain occurs, the opposite is best: a cold pack wrapped in a towel will help to reduce swelling.

Sore lips, a sore mouth and mouth ulcers often appear as the result of too much lip activity, such as changing to piccolo, alto or bass flute often, or extended techniques. A salt water mouthwash will often calm it down overnight.

USING ANTI-PERSPIRANT

This can be very effective to prevent the lip plate or grip on the flute, but *only* if sprayed on the fingers and then applied to the chin. *Never* directly spray your face or lip.

The long-term solution is the have the part of the lip-plate against the lip engraved. A cheaper and easier option has already been discussed in Section 1.5, *Lip plate insecurity*.

THE USE OF DRUGS

The most common drugs used to temporarily help someone suffering from stage nerves are beta-blockers, widely prescribed for heart disorders. They work by preventing a chemical in the brain from triggering and releasing adrenaline, the substance which causes the nerves to twitch, the legs and hands to shake and generally causes us to feel uncomfortable. Centuries ago, adrenaline was necessary to help primitive man run away faster or fight danger more successfully. In a concert, it is just plain annoying! A doctor will generally prescribe and allow the use of beta-blockers for occasional use. This is better than the unwanted stress in a performance. They are non-addictive and after a few uses can often be dispensed with as the player gains in confidence. There are other solutions favoured by performers including non-drugs, health products and even various kinds of drinks for those who prefer non-drug use.

The choice is yours.

4

Section 4

4.1 TEACHING STRATEGIES

SETTING UP AS A TEACHER

It has been said that teaching cannot be taught. On checking the local teacher training college curriculum a few years back, I noticed that the subject of 'How to Teach' was not covered, though it did include the 'History of Education', the 'Psychology of Teaching' and other such subjects. The trainee teacher can pick up many interesting ideas, however successfully communicating them in a motivating way is a special gift that you won't learn simply from undertaking a college degree.

This section aims to guide young or inexperienced teachers by focussing on peripheral but important matters.

When starting out as a private teacher you should be realistic about your goals — a good reputation takes time to establish. Your students may not blossom overnight, and it may take some years before your name and reputation become a byword for good lessons.

FEES

A good start is to find out what other teachers charge locally and use this as a guide. It is important not to undervalue yourself. Compare your skills with those of other teachers — qualifications, experience, masterclasses, study abroad, etc.

I remember the famous flutist Julius Baker (1915–2003) telling me about his parents' search for a flute teacher in the local directory when he was young. Of the three people listed, his parents discarded the cheapest on the grounds that the lessons wouldn't be any good. Of course, this doesn't follow, but people generally respect a higher fee as the teacher is most likely to be of greater value, silly though that might be.

ESTABLISHING A TEACHING CONTRACT AND ADVISING PARENTS

When starting a teaching career, you should consider setting out a contract for students which can be either detailed or quite simple. A contract will help to avoid later disputes.

The contract should be headed with full contact details, followed by the half-hourly rate and schedule of lessons.

A policy for cancellations should be agreed in advance. For example:

- If the teacher or student cancels a lesson, it will be made up when convenient, providing two or more days' notice is given. If less notice is given, the lesson will be forfeited.

- Lessons are arranged in a series of ten. Only in exceptional circumstances will shorter periods or single lessons be considered.

- The fee for a series of lessons must be paid for in advance.

Some teachers may wish to set out every eventuality, such as the notice period for cancellation and the proportion of fees to be refunded. Generally, parents might appreciate a simpler set of rules making clear the agreement between both of you in advance. Some teachers might insist that parents sign and return a copy of the contract, though this is perhaps too fussy and best avoided.

A single isolated lesson with a new student can prove problematic. Criticism, however constructive, may not be absorbed and put into practice without a second lesson, as the new student may not follow your advice. A more experienced teacher may offer an 'advice audition', during which they listen to the student play and then discuss with them career options, colleges, universities and perhaps teachers too. This kind of audition is helpful as you can be completely honest. Instrumental teachers may also offer music theory and aural tuition as part of the lesson.

The points listed above should be considered and altered depending on personal and local circumstances; each teacher will have their own idea of what is fair and reasonable. If you are still in doubt, you could ask other local instrumental teachers for their advice.

Some parents seem to think that lessons alone are enough. Point out that you can only guide the student, and that they must do the work in order for progress to be made. Insist that the parents make time for the student to practise free of TV, video games, phones and the like. It is essential for students to have a quiet place to practise. Encourage them to practise standing up.

Advise the parents to invest in a few useful accessories. They should use a music stand to help their posture and comfort, rather than propping the music up on a table. A mirror can further aid with posture and embouchure improvement. The student should also obtain a metronome and tuner — there are plenty available, including apps. A good pencil and eraser will also be useful.

METHOD BOOKS

There are many hundreds of tutor books and suitable beginner repertoire currently in print in several languages. The selection is truly staggering. Some use popular music, play-along CDs, illustrations, cartoons and further digital content in an effort to enhance the book. Strip away all the peripheral and popular stuff and we are left with three basic methods of learning the flute:

- **The simple diatonic method** teaches the notes B, A, G, F, E, D and C2 in that order, followed by the second octave. The student will eventually learn the chromatic notes F♯, G♯ and C♯. This is the most common method.

- **The chromatic method** introduces almost all the notes of the first octave from the outset.

- **The third method** embraces popular traditional melodies rather than teaching notes first. Folk tunes, tunes from Bollywood movies and even pop songs are used to get the student playing tunes from the outset.

The simple diatonic method allows the student to learn most of the notes in easy keys in a comparatively short time — perhaps at the cost of a good tone — however, this can enable the student to participate in ensembles sooner than other methods. It might use popular melodies or even national tunes to make the learning process more amenable. There are hundreds of books that use this approach, and they often come with play-along CDs and even videos.

The chromatic method is a long-term scheme designed to get the student performing well, and takes years rather than weeks. This lays down solid foundations, and this will show later in their development. There are relatively few publications that follow this method: Marcel Moyse wrote the first, *Le Débutant Flûtiste* (The Beginner Flutist), and the other is the *Practice Book for Beginners* written by myself. Both approaches are similar: the player first learns B, A and G, followed by G♯, F and E, and then F♯. This paves the way for simple tunes but also allows melodies to be played in A minor, E major, etc. — a rather novel way to begin. The beginner student learns to play in unusual keys quite early on, which can be a great advantage for them in their progression. They also stay in the lower register for longer, establishing a good low-register tone quality. This sets the foundation for tone building, and develops confidence in performing across all keys.

Both the first and second methods have their fans, and I have written books which embrace both methods.

The third method involves the use of books with simple, current, popular repertoire and quick-fix solutions, with little thought to long-term development. There may also be distracting imagery and backing audio.

Academic correctness might take a back seat but the player soon learns a few simple melodies — which was perhaps all they set out to achieve when they first decided to play.

Having read the above, it is obvious which method the author prefers. Preference might depend on regional tradition, with some methods being more prevalent than others, and will certainly vary from teacher to teacher and student to student.

How do you decide which is right for you and your student? You should think about this question:

Are you teaching the student to become
proficient next week, or the year after next?

Most young players would prefer to learn quickly, with the goal of playing in the school band or orchestra as soon as possible. A complete beginner naturally has little conception of what their future might hold; they may simply want to play a few popular tunes to amuse themselves. You should use whichever method is best for your student, and you may even try combining several to achieve these goals.

There are many options when it comes to trying out these methods. You may benefit from exploring your local music book store to seek out the most well-liked, completely unknown, or entirely new books to help you and your student develop. Some teachers prefer to use a selection of different books of similar methods just to provide a change from routine or to fill in what they feel is missing from other books.

I spent twelve years teaching beginners and used a mixture of books depending on what seemed to be the most suitable for each student. There is a huge variety of methods to choose from, and it may benefit both the teacher and student to experiment with the options.

Students can benefit from learning by imitation or aspiration, so consider playing to them often during the lessons.

TEACHING IN GROUPS

Group tuition is often popular with parents as it cuts costs, but this can be quite tough for the teacher, and there are major disadvantages. As an example, with a group of four, the weakest will likely have more time spent on them than the others. A good solution is to suggest that this student occasionally takes private lessons. Alternatively, the teacher should keep lesson progression within reasonable expectations, given the size of the group. Though it's likely to be slower in a group lesson, individuals may learn from one another and find encouragement from their classmates.

This approach to teaching is more common in school environments, however it's possible to also teach groups of adults in this way. Regardless of age, group learning will develop ensemble skills — key to improving all-round musicianship — and can help to boost enthusiasm and confidence.

TEACHING MATURE STUDENTS

The motivations behind an adult taking up an instrument are many and varied: quite often they feel they missed out when at school. Some want to be able to play pieces with their children, and others with older children (now taking up less of their time) want to learn for the sheer pleasure of it, and perhaps to join the local amateur band or orchestra. Adults don't have the short arms and posture difficulties that young children have, so setting a good posture and hand position is fairly easy. Older beginners may struggle with a variety of issues: breathing, tremor, arthritis or other problems which may interfere with their progression.

Experienced teachers of adults seem to agree that the fingering 'rules' set for younger players need not apply so strictly for adults. This is not to imply that they are taught bad habits, but that mature players are much less likely to want to pursue a musical career, and so easier fingerings, (such as using the right-hand second finger for F♯) can be allowed.

Adults sometimes have problems memorising fingerings and may get confused or use them incorrectly. To help with holding the flute securely, you might suggest the application of first aid plasters under the right thumb and left-hand first finger. There is further similar advice in Section 1.5, *Open-hole difficulties*.

With older players, standing up to practise may be difficult, and it could be better for them to sit, provided they are given proper instruction regarding posture and position.

Some adults may grow impatient or frustrated when progress begins to slow; some expect to sound wonderful after just a few weeks. You can help by growing their knowledge around the music itself. Discuss theory, key signatures, history, and other matters as they come up in the music

TEACHING THE VERY YOUNG

There is no reason at all not to seriously consider the 'fife' as a practical flute for a very young or small person. The stretch of the hands on a normal flute is too much for a small body, and if someone really wants to start that young then the fife is a good place to begin. I can recommend the fife and fife method marketed by Liz Goodwin, and fifes manufactured by Yamaha, Aulos, Nuvo and Guo. Some of these are sold together with a suitable book including fingering advice, which will make the job much easier.

Some flutes are made with a curved or bent head joint, shortening the length of the instrument and allowing for a near-normal hand position. The tone of these are perfectly acceptable, though perhaps not completely satisfactory for a professional player. These flutes are not a new development: an upright flute was first made commercially in Italy during the middle of the 19th Century. The drawing of the upright head joint (below, *c.* 1860) is by Boehm himself, despite some modern-day manufacturers claiming this as their own invention.

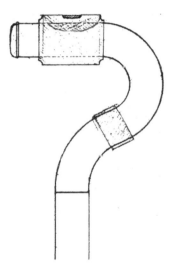

An original Theobald Boehm drawing from the Munich Municipal Archive, Germany.
Supplied by Ludwig Boehm
Fig. 4.1

Those who regularly teach the very young say that music-based games and competitions with prizes can stimulate the children to practise. The use of popular stickers, rewards and practice charts may help too.

Very young players need a shorter time for lessons, but if this is not feasible then diversions can be effective. Sometimes a music history lesson can be just as engaging and enlightening as a practical lesson.

'Panpipes', the 'nai' or 'nay', the 'kena' or 'quena', the simple north Indian-style 'bansuri' and bamboo pipes and whistles of all kinds are all interesting instruments found in the Far East, Middle East and India. Search online or in books for interesting pictures, or find videos of these amazing instruments in action. The very best of teachers might even source one of these instruments to show at the lesson!

WHAT KIND OF TEACHER?

There are many different types of teacher. The two extremes are broadly outlined below with the prospective teacher's career philosophy somewhere between the two.

1. **The therapist**. This teacher will teach anyone who wants to play, regardless of talent or performing problems. As a teacher declared some years ago, *'If someone wants to play the flute, I will do everything to help them, even if they show little aptitude'*. Aptitude problems include pitch, rhythm and co-ordination difficulties, as well as a lack of musicality. A teacher once stated: *'If a child has some problems, isn't it better they spend their time doing something more rewarding? If after some years of learning, surely a performance of a slow movement of a Handel sonata played badly does not justify the time and money spent practising an instrument for which they have little or no talent?'*

2. **The selective teacher**. This teacher will only help someone who has a reasonable talent. The 'minimal talent' is a level set by teachers individually, however there may be exceptions, depending on the circumstances. Of course, no one draws a line beyond which they will not budge and it is clear that the 'line' is a very broad one.

4.2 SETTING UP A TEACHING SPACE

Some teachers prefer to set up a designated room where the students come for lessons and group ensembles and visiting teacher classes may also be possible. Obviously, the most important feature is having a noise-free place in which to set it up. It is also useful to have a piano available, even an electronic one. Recording and playback equipment can be very useful for playing back a track to help illustrate a point. A recording device or app can be used to record lessons. A computer, tablet or mobile phone can be used to make lesson notes to be mailed to the student later as a reminder.

In these times, mobile phones and tablets can provide useful apps for many purposes. As mentioned before, there are metronomes available as well as all kinds of ear training and music theory apps. Mention should also be made of the *Amazing Slow Downer* app. This is great if the student needs to hear the piece slower to understand the pulse and rhythm or play with an accompaniment at a slower speed.

If you have other members in your house to consider, a consultation with them is essential as students may wish to use the house toilet or the kitchen for water, not to mention the storage of wet clothing, umbrellas and boots in bad weather. Others living with you may object to this.

If such a space was suitably equipped, it could be hired out to other instrumental teachers too.

Each country has its own laws and practices regarding who can be taught at home. For example, some cities may require that the teacher has a criminal check, particularly if teaching youngsters, and some require that the teacher obtain certificates in emergency first aid and CPR. It is also worth considering getting liability insurance.

CLASS LESSONS

The merit of masterclass learning cannot be underestimated, providing that a few guidelines are followed. The first is that the attendees should not be treated as bystanders but as listeners who are taking a limited but active part. This is how all great classes are conducted. The next is that the teacher should always address the class, rather than the performer. That way, the listeners feel that they are part of the class rather than merely onlookers. Thirdly, the choice of pieces being performed should be sent to the participants in advance so that they can bring along a copy of the work being played. This last guideline may also arouse interest in a comparison of different editions.

The 'whole class' concept helps the players to get used to playing in front of each other and deals with nerves too. If regular classes are not possible, even an occasional class will help with this and can also be used as a social occasion.

Visiting teachers could be invited to give a class in a related subject such as the recorder, Baroque flute, piccolo, or alto and bass flutes.

A TEACHING LIBRARY

A well-equipped space should have a library of flute books, perhaps not for borrowing but for showing examples to the students. The Bibliography at the end of this book shows examples. A loan library of simple pieces to help the less well-off may also be a possibility. This can be expensive unless time is spent repairing damaged music and noting who has taken what away. As troublesome as this might seem, it does speed up the learning process to have a suitable melody or piece immediately available when needed, without waiting for it to be posted or obtained from a shop. The National Flute Association of the USA has a selected repertoire list which is also very useful.

4.3 PRACTICE PLANS

PRACTICE PLANS FOR STUDENTS

Whatever the age of your student, a practice schedule of some kind can be helpful to them and can range from a programme of 20 minutes to two hours or more. Whatever time is available, an outline of what needs to be practised can be helpful. A typical schedule might contain a few minutes of tone practice, followed by a technical exercise that focuses on a particular problem, then scales and a tune, finishing with a study or piece. As mentioned earlier, articulation is always best done in small chunks of a few minutes, several times an hour. For the best possible outcome, encourage the idea of *daily* practice.

Encourage older and more experienced students to get into the habit of practising from the piano part, if there is one. The piano score shows all the details of the piece and, whether or not they play the piano, the shapes of the notes underneath and the rhythms will help to give some idea of what part the piano plays in the performance. This helps enormously in performing intelligently and expressing the music set out by the composer. Experienced juries will say that they are aware when a player 'knows' the accompanying part, whether it is a chamber ensemble, an orchestra or a piano. It shows up in a performance.

Encourage them not to listen to recordings when learning a new piece, as it may result in copying what they hear others doing. It is far better to first look at the music and try to understand what the composer is portraying — how all parts fit together and the different roles of the instrument, within the composition — before then listening to another player, and their understanding of the composer's intentions.

PRACTICE PLANS FOR TEACHERS

A few minutes of practice a day can work wonders in keeping up a teacher's level of playing. When the teacher's highlight of the week is performing the second flute part of 'Row, Row, Row Your Boat' with the first part played badly out of tune, the teacher's own standard of playing can easily slip back, unknowingly. Many times, I have heard teachers bewail the fact that they hadn't realised that their playing level had slipped so far, and perhaps this was because they hadn't kept up-to-date with what's going on in the flute world.

One useful tip is to make a point of attending a masterclass or summer camp for flutists, with a well-known player, at least once a year. Most conventions feature helpful lectures and discussions on teaching and related subjects. Attending a flute convention can also help to bring a teacher up-to-date with emerging talent, books, methods, flutes, innovations — including daft ones — and repertoire, as well as meeting others in the same teaching situation. Another way to keep up with new repertoire is to look at examination board syllabuses for new music ideas.

Joining the National Flute Society or similar associations will keep the teacher aware of what is new in the society's journal, essential in finding new repertoire, methods, and the latest flute gadgets. Online flute discussion lists are also helpful, and there are many out there. They cost nothing, yet can be a great source of information.

Always making a point of going to flute recitals where possible, another good way of keeping up with what is happening in our flute world.

4.4 STUDENT PERFORMING PROBLEMS

At a teacher's seminar some years ago, the speaker invited questions from the audience with the caveat, *'Please do not start your question with, "I once had a student who..." because we have all had students like this!'*. It seems there are as many aberrations in teaching as there are students. That apart, all teachers will have come across students with rhythm and pitch problems, and even some who appear to have 'no musicality'. The last is beyond this book to deal with, though I may have solutions for the other two, listed below. Occasionally, students may decide to seek internet guidance instead of following your advice. As someone once remarked, *'There are some... and some'*.

RHYTHM PROBLEMS

Rhythm (or 'having rhythm') can be defined either as 'the forward flow of music' or, less artistically, as 'the ability to accurately predict a future point in time'. It is the second definition which mostly concerns the teacher. There are tests using recorded 'bleeps' to which the student responds, as well as online rhythm 'trainers'. What is clear from research is that most rhythm problems can be improved.

More useful to the teacher may be the following test which I devised many years ago — it can be done during the lesson without any previous preparation.

Both teacher and student should sit at a table with their elbows and arms resting on it, holding a pencil or pen with the solid end for use as a tapping tool. The teacher will either use a metronome set at 60 beats per minute or provide a stable beat themselves by tapping the table with the pencil.

The student is then asked to:

1. Listen for a few moments to the beat, and then to tap *exactly* in time with it.

2. Repeat this with their eyes closed — this is so that they cannot observe your pencil movement or the metronome. *Note any inaccuracy.*

3. Continue tapping at *exactly the same speed* after the teacher has stopped. *Note any inaccuracy.*

4. Start tapping again with the teacher and after a few seconds, ask them to tap only *every other one* of your beats. Then, the teacher will stop tapping, but the student will continue. *Tapping very slowly with big gaps between taps is much more difficult.*

5. Ask them to tap every beat as before but tell them you will try to distract them by tapping other rhythms. After a few moments of tapping together, you will tap *every other beat* to begin with; then tap exactly *between* the students beats; then triplets *between* the beats.

6. Finally, while they are trying hard to maintain their regularity of beat, try tapping randomly to try to put them off.

When this has been completed, the teacher will have observed whether the student has been able to stay strictly in time, even though there were beats missing and the teacher was deliberately trying to put them off. Although this little test can help determine if the student has weak sense of rhythm, more importantly, the teacher should observe the student's body language and the movement of their arm and hand using the pencil! A student who is unsure, or may have a weakness here, will tap with less determination, perhaps because they are not *exactly* sure where the beat will fall. Their arm or wrist may move in an indeterminate way, in other words, they may not be able to *accurately* predict where the beat will fall and their arm movement reflects this. If there seems to be a rhythm problem, the reader may be glad to know that rhythm can be improved though the student needs to understand that only by their own efforts might any improvement take place..

Ultimately, a good rhythm must come from themselves, rather than an external source, but to begin with, for a short time each day, they should play with the metronome and tap their foot at the same time. Foot-tapping can be irritating to those around them, but the creation of rhythm from within themselves will eventually lead to a stronger rhythmic sense. Here are some other suggestions:

- Obtain a non-digital clock, the kind which ticks reasonably loudly and needs winding up. This should be placed beside the student's bed for them to listen to, and perhaps to hum tunes to before sleeping.

- Use 'taps' on the heels of their shoes so that walking makes an audible sound to which they can hum tunes. Taps can easily be added to shoes, even soft shoes.

- Use finger nails to tap out rhythms when listening to music or watching TV.

- Take up dancing — it might help.

Progress may be slow, but this should eventually help with their sense of rhythm, especially with syncopated notes. Their chance of improving depends on their awareness of the problem as well as their determination to get better.

PITCH AND TUNING DIFFICULTIES

This subject is divided into two sections: one for those who have difficulties hearing or adjusting to intervals smaller than a semitone, and one for those who have difficulties with keys, such as hearing intervals, key changes, or the even the differences between major and minor keys.

For those students who have trouble with small intervals, this may be obvious when adjusting the pitch during tuning. It might also show when trying to play in tune with other instruments, such as the piano.

Tests such as those set out by Carl Seashore measure a subject's ability to hear 50 pairs of notes in which the second note is either higher or lower than the first. As the 50 pairs of notes progress, the interval between them diminishes until there is only a very small interval between the two. Studies suggest that if the student's score is poor, there is really nothing that can be done to improve it. This ability would be much more important to a string player, particularly a violinist. A flutist does not need so sensitive an ear to be able to fix the ever-problematic C#2, for example, and a sensitive ear is not vital for most students, particularly those not following a professional career.

Those students having difficulties with larger intervals can attend ear training sessions at colleges where other subjects such as keyboard harmony will also help a great deal.

The reader may like to know that I tested a new intake of students at a prestigious music college in the UK using Seashore's *Pitch Discrimination* and *Tonal Memory* tests. The same students were tested again three years later after they had undergone rigorous training and first rate lessons. Interestingly, the results of the second test were very similar, even after three years of chamber music, wind and string ensembles, and keyboard harmony classes, as well as private lessons with famous soloists. On the second testing, a very few had left college during the past three years; they were almost entirely those with low scores in the Pitch Test.

INTERPRETATION

To help students of all ages to perform well, a good start is to teach them that musical structure is well-ordered and disciplined. The construction of most tunes and melodies is a 'two-bar, two-bar and four-bar' formula, usually repeated. This simple formula can be expanded to construct a short piece: A is the melody, B is counter melody, A is a repeat of the first melody again and finishes with a *coda*. It may also have an introduction. The Moyse *24 Little Melodious Studies* are excellent examples of the 16- and 32-bar formula. Understanding this will help the student appreciate how to build a melodic structure when performing.

Teachers should explain or demonstrate this structure theory, as it greatly affects both the dynamics and the interpretation of a piece. It will help the student to gain a better understanding of tunes, movements of sonatas and much of our well-known flute repertoire.

There are plenty more examples of exercises in Moyse's *Tone Development Through Interpretation*.

The construction and practice of melodies have already been detailed for the student in Section 2.2, *Melodies*.

TEACHING EXPRESSION

This involves two related techniques; encouraging loud and soft playing, coupled with controlling the pitch. Of course, just to encourage playing softly inevitably means that the pitch will drop. When to introduce how to control the pitch varies from student to student, but a good sign is when they appear to want to be expressive, either in their playing or in bodily movement. The second of the *Practice Book for Beginners* (Novello) does provide an introduction to this technique quite early on. It will give the beginner a basic understanding of expression from the outset, rather than introducing it later as a special technique.

TEACHING VIBRATO

When to introduce this varies a great deal from person to person. It might be considered an advanced technique, though I have observed an occasional young student trying to emulate another performer. Whenever it is taught, once the teacher can hear attempts to produce a wobble in the tone, that is the moment in which it *must* be addressed. There are many players who wish the correct technique had been acquired at this stage, rather than learning a defective vibrato which is almost always very difficult to remedy. The correct learning procedure is set out in *Practice Book Four* (Novello).

4.5 FUN STUFF

For younger students, it is useful to have a handful of 'fun exercises' to hold their attention whilst learning. It is not difficult to teach them some contemporary flute techniques such as multiphonics (see Section 3.7, *Multiphonics*).

Another easy technique to try is double stopping by adding the first and second trill keys to F2:

Double Stopping
Fig. 4.3

With the head joint detached, they can play a glissando by moving their finger in and out of the tube. Then, they can try to play melodies by placing their finger in the end of the head joint at different increments.

Whilst the head joint is out, they might try playing the body vertically as like the native South American instrument, *quena* or *kena*. The barrel is held against the lip and should be half-covered to get the body to sound. The scale is rather strange!

Upright Playing
Fig. 4.4

If they are a more advanced player, they might also try either flutter tonguing or playing and singing at the same time. If someone is good at this, they might try playing a tune and singing the bass line (see *Practice Book Four*, page 14, 'Trios for Two Flutes').

Turning the head joint upside down on the flute and then playing it on the top lip can be fun too. It takes a little time to get accustomed to blowing it upside down, but some players can make it sound really convincing with a little practice.

Just as an occasional and amusing diversion, a group could try playing the same tune with one hand on another person's flute as shown below. The second and third students have their right hands on the flute in front.

A Funny Trio
Fig. 4.2

A small group can try linking arms, like the players in Fig. 4.5, and if they are close to the same height, they can do this in an informal concert.

Friends
Fig. 4.5

When you have exhausted all the fun ways to play the flute, you could show them this flute below, for interest. It is made from a human tibia, a copy of a bone found in Germany in 1953, and was made about 10,000 years ago. This is how it all began!

The Bone
Fig. 4.6

A thought...

How does the flute compare with the other woodwinds in learning difficulty? Your author taught the oboe, clarinet and bassoon for some years at state schools. The oboe is certainly more difficult, not just the reed, but the fingering with its 'pinhole key' under the 1st finger left hand (similar to our C#2 to G#2), not to mention the 'forked F'.

Similarly, some bassoons respond differently in the upper register, and alternative fingerings should be explored to find the best solution for the player's instrument. The left thumb is extremely active, often operating six or seven notes by itself. No mention will be made to the size and weight of the case!

The clarinet is easier, though the 'break' always causes a slow-down in learning as the instrument does not overblow an octave. It has the same fingering as our D2 on the flute, but on releasing the 'register key', with the same fingering, it drops down a 12th to low G. An octave plus a fifth has to be played with the same number of fingers...

The flute is an easy instrument. Just keep reminding yourself. I still remember the virtuoso French flutist, Alain Marion saying, *'The flute is so easy. That's why I play it!'*

5

Section 5

5.1 EAR TRAINING, PLAYING IN TUNE, FLUTE TUNING AND REPAIRS

INTRODUCTION

At college and university, ear training is taught using intervals, chord recognition, transposition, and dictation. This section is concerned with playing in tune as a soloist or an ensemble player. The ear training section here will deal with intervals smaller than a semitone.

Pitch distinction varies widely from person to person. Very few are able to distinguish extremely fine pitch variations of a cent or two. Perfect pitch is an exceptional ability where the person can distinguish, say, between 440.1Hz and 440.2Hz. Perfect pitch is the rare but natural ability to accurately name the pitch of a random note on first hearing, whereas relative pitch relies on pitch memory in relation to other pitches. This is not uncommon.

There are a few things you can do to check and improve your ability:

1. Measure your pitch discrimination ability. There are tests which can measure this and will help in your decision making later. They are set out below (and in Section 4.4, *Pitch and tuning difficulties*).

2. Examine your flute and the scale to which it was built.

3. Finally, play some simple melodies to test out and practise your new skills.

SHARPENING YOUR EARS

Piano tuners naturally have a very fine sense of pitch discrimination and, if you know one, they will confirm that after a break of a week or more, they need to re-sharpen their pitch sense. After lack of use, it seems that most people's ability to hear very small differences in pitch declines, but there are some exercises that can be done to bring back the ear's ability to hear these fine distinctions once again.

You will need a good-quality piano which is well in tune, preferably a grand or baby grand, though a good-quality upright piano can do the job quite well. If it is a grand, open the lid fully. It might also be helpful to remove the music rest which usually slides out of the front. If it is an upright piano, raise the top lid and take out the front panel and music rest by turning the two wooden clips to be found at each end inside of the front, so that it can be removed. This makes it much easier to hear.

Now play the exercises below on the piano. They should help to sharpen your perception of pitch. You will need a quiet environment.

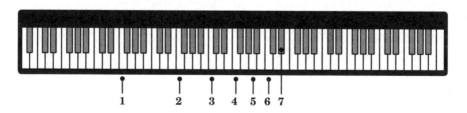

Fig 5.1

Play low F, as shown as '1', above. If this note sounds in tune without any wavering or sourness, then that's fine. If it does not, choose another nearby note such as G or A. Listen for a clear, in-tune note. There are likely to be two strings struck inside the piano when sounding these notes and they must both agree with each other.

Let us assume your F *is* in tune. Play it again, holding the key down until the sound disappears. How many other notes did you hear? Repeat this a few times if you wish to make sure.

With your right hand, place your finger gently down on the F one octave higher than the F you have just played, shown above. Do this *without* allowing the hammer to strike the string — just take the damper off the string without making a sound. *Without letting go of this F key,* with your left hand, strike the original low F, *forte*. Wait a couple of seconds and then, still holding down the higher octave, release the low F. You should hear a faint F an octave higher, the result of the lower F's second harmonic forcing the higher F strings to sound 'in sympathy'. This is known as *sympathetic vibration.*

Repeat the exercise for the third harmonic, C. Gently press down C a 12th above the low F without sounding the note. When low F is sounded *forte*, then released, its third harmonic, C, should be heard moderately loudly. Now play a loud F and listen for the third harmonic, C, within the tone of the note. Repeat this a few times until you can hear the C clearly. Remind yourself that the C has always been there but what has changed is your *awareness* of it.

The harmonic series on F is set out below:

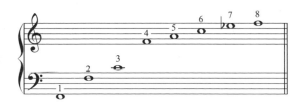

The harmonic series on F
Fig. 5.2

Repeat this exercise by taking the damper off F, two octaves higher than the low F arrowed as '4'. The *sympathetic vibration* may not produce such a strong note. This is because the harmonics are not equally strong within a note. Now with your right hand, hold down A, no. '5', the fifth harmonic of low F *without it sounding*, then play the low F again loudly and after a couple of seconds, release that key. You will probably hear only a faint A, if at all. This is because the low F string is producing a flatter fifth harmonic A, not at the pitch the piano's upper A is tuned to. This discovery tells us that for two flutes to play a true major third, the upper note must be played flatter. This 'out-of-tuneness' is the reason that thirds are *major* or *minor* and not 'perfect'. In the interval of a perfect fifth, we have two thirds, one small and one large, or one minor and one major. The difference between them is a little over a quarter of a tone. Spend a little time listening to the fifth harmonic of F, the A, because you will be asked to listen to it in your own tone later. More importantly, when you practise the flute, you might also try playing major thirds at this slightly flatter pitch too. There will be more about this later.

Continue up the harmonic series from F to the sixth harmonic, C, which may be very faint. Then on to the seventh harmonic, E♭, which will not produce a sympathetic tone because the natural harmonic is so flat and nowhere near the E♭ seventh the piano is tuned to, or that we are accustomed to hearing.

By this time, your ear will have become more aware and you will be hearing the harmonics, perhaps for the first time.

Play the low F again loudly and listen to the fifth harmonic, in effect, a major third. Before the harmonic chord has faded away and without letting go the key, softly play a few notes of an F minor chord. The harmony should clash badly because you are, in effect, playing two chords, F minor and F major together. Think about this!

It is interesting that, centuries ago, some monks who were singing together disliked the sound of a minor chord because they could also hear the fifth harmonic (the major third) of the bass note at the same time as the minor third which they were singing. One monk suggested that they change minor chords to major chords, sharpening the third when the chord was a long one such as at a cadence. They did this and liked it! The monastery where they lived was in Picardy, Northern France and these were known as *Picardy Thirds*. (In French, singular: *Tierce de Picardie*).

The famous orchestral passage below typifies the intonation problem of thirds, familiar to many flute players.

Mendelssohn: Overture to A Midsummer Night's Dream.
Fig. 5.3

Incidentally, when playing a loud low note on the piano, as you have been doing with low F, notice that the seventh harmonic, E♭, takes almost a second or more to sound. This is because the piano maker has arranged that the hammer will strike the string one-seventh of the way along its length, or multiples of this figure. This is to prevent the irritating seventh harmonic from sounding too soon. Some say that you can tell a well-made and good-toned piano by the length of time it takes for the seventh harmonic to sound: the longer it takes, the better the piano. Usually, but not always, bigger classy pianos have almost a two-second delay before the seventh harmonic sounds.

Finally, let us sensitise our ears to the harmonics in our own flute tone. Think of the flute tone as a recipe, where a note consists of a *fundamental* (or first harmonic) and four or more harmonics above it. The relative strength of these other harmonics gives different tone colours; these vary from player to player, enabling us perhaps to identify the individual. The flute has about five harmonics and the difference between one player and another is the relative strength of them: one player may have a reedy tone which may indicate a strong second harmonic, the octave. Another player might have a hollow tone, perhaps indicating a weaker second and possibly third harmonic. It is worth noting in passing that both the oboe and the violin have around twelve or thirteen harmonics, but each instrument produces them at different strengths enabling us to tell the difference between the two instruments. We further distinguish instruments by how each note begins, whether bowed, tongued or struck, and as they change from one to another. Each 'first' sound is known as a *starting transient*. We could say that the oboe and the violin have the same ingredients, but in different quantities and different starting transients..

Now, take up your flute and play low D with a hollow, soft tone colour. This means to play with a strong fundamental or first harmonic and weak second. Listen for the third harmonic, A2. This might take some adjustments of tone and intonation as this harmonic isn't always apparent. You can play it as a whistle tone, if you like, just to check its pitch, but the idea here is to hear the note as part of your tone. Though this may take time to hear, remember that these harmonics are always there but need care and patience to hear them.

Playing *really well* in tune means being aware of the bass and the other parts of a chord so as to adjust your own pitch and play closer to *just intonation*. If a piano were tuned to *just intonation,* it would only be possible to play in two or three keys. To play in all keys equally, the piano must be tuned with equal semitones so that, although the intervals are not quite 'correct', the result is not unpleasing.

Throughout history, musicians have tried to find a compromise between *equal temperament* and *just intonation*. For today's performer, we have arrived at a point where it is important to play firstly in *equal temperament,* and then, if our ear and technique allows, to alter some intervals so that we play better in tune and sound more expressive. This technique will also serve the performer very well in an orchestra where the ability to be flexible is of great importance.

Harpsichord players sometimes ask for their instrument to be tuned to a particular 'temperament', that is to say that they do not want it tuned to *equal temperament*, with equally spaced semitones, but to a compromise temperament or scale. They may ask for this for early music performances. This means that the few keys to be used in the piece may have flatter major thirds, but will sound fine. Of course, more remote keys are not possible, with some intervals sounding badly out of tune. They ask for these special scales because they know that the 'early' music they are going to perform will not wander far from the 'home key'.

Historically, there have been many such temperaments. The book *Tuning the Historical Temperaments by Ear* contains 256 different temperaments, or ways to tune a keyboard instrument to avoid equal temperament. Some of these have strange names such as the *Andreas Werkmeister No. 3,* obviously set out by him. Some also have very long titles such as *The Theoretically Correct 5/66 Ditonic (sic) Comma Temperament as Altered by J.G. Neidhardt in His '5th Circle No. 4' in the Original Position.* That is certainly a mouthful, but why bother with these curiosities? Well, the result does sound more beautiful, but only with 'early' music which modulates to fewer keys with its simpler chords and progressions. The listener, too, needs to become used to these temperaments in order to really appreciate them. It's a little like trying perfumes, tasting teas or even wine tasting!

EXAMINING YOUR FLUTE

We will now take a look at the flute itself. Has it been correctly tuned to equal temperament? If not, or you have no idea if it has, then is there anything that can be done? These questions will be answered first as all the later work on intonation will naturally rely on you working with a correctly tuned flute.

We commonly refer to the tone hole positions on our flutes, relative to each other, as *the scale*. In 2013, the *scales* from six famous-brand flutes were carefully measured using electronic callipers. This tool can accurately measure the position of the centre of each tone hole from the end of the foot of the flute. The resulting figures from each flute were set out and compared. *All the scales were different, not one flute agreeing with another.* This seems to imply that flute makers presume there are different versions of equal temperament. Why the flute scales were different from each other is not known. Some were so different that we must assume that some had tone holes positioned in incorrect places.

Some manufacturers claim that individual notes should be tuned by the player. Again, this is true, and something we do to fix any discordant notes, but why should we tune notes which have been incorrectly placed on our flutes by the maker? It is easy to argue that each maker has their own idea of flute scales, but we are discussing *equal temperament*. There is only one version of *equal temperament*, no matter which instrument is measured, and to have six or more versions is absurd. I recently bought eight different brands of plastic and wooden rulers and placed them side by side. The inches and centimetres all agreed. Just suppose those rulers were shown to have different distances between the inches or centimetres and perhaps even the total length of the ruler differed as well — then where would we be? We rely on a standard set of measurements for science, maths and engineering as well as in cooking and medicine, but not, it seems, in flute making!

Good intonation relies on equal temperament — the division of the octave into 12 equal semitones outlined by the Chinese court astronomer, historian, physicist and mathematician, Zhu Zaiyu, Prince of Zheng of the Ming Dynasty in 1584.

Everyone plays the flute differently, but experience has shown that almost every player uses roughly the same flute length. It follows that the length of a flute and its scale should suit all of us.

We will move on to a plan for checking your own flute and if necessary, making small alterations to make it easier for you to play in tune. It is not essential to take any action now, but just reading what is to follow will help in understanding why it may be necessary. This section may also add to your knowledge of flute scales and tuning in general.

FLUTE SCALES

Musicians are well-known to dislike maths, perhaps even having an absolute aversion to it. That's fine. What is set out below is an easy way for you to understand how flutes scales are made. This will help you in the future and, if necessary, help you to make important decisions about your own flute.

A simple way to begin is to use the guitar as a model, as it is easier to visualise. To set the position of the frets on a guitar — or the tone holes on a flute — an *octave length* must first be determined. This is simply calculating the total length of one octave on the guitar fingerboard (or the flute tube) before adding frets (or tone holes).

Let us imagine the manufacturer has completed the body and neck of a guitar and now needs to add the frets. They *can* do this by simply placing frets where they seem to be correct and moving them about until the tuning seems right. This would take a lot of time and may still result in a badly-tuned instrument.

The easy way is to place a string on the instrument and tune it to, for example, C, and slide the finger up the fingerboard until the exact octave C above is obtained; a mark is made here. The distance between the 'nut' — where the string effectively begins at the top of the guitar — and the mark just made on the fingerboard showing the octave is carefully measured. This is termed the *octave length*. The *octave length* arrived at by guitar manufacturers is in the region of 325mm, at A = 440Hz.

So far, we have a guitar with two Cs: C_1 and its octave, C_2. Between these two points, the rest of a chromatic scale needs to be determined.

To do this, the *octave length* of 325mm must first be doubled to give the *sounding length* of 650mm. We double the octave length because, if you look at your flute, the finger holes take up about half of the total length of the flute.

After centuries of lute and guitar making, the makers agreed that the *sounding length* should be divided by 17.834. This figure was found by experiment, though a few guitar makers do use the figure of 18.0, perhaps for simplicity.

The picture below shows a comparison between the flute tone holes and guitar fingerboard.

Comparison: frets and tone holes
Fig. 5.4

The next step is to divide the *sounding length,* 650.0mm, by 17.834; using your calculator, this shows a figure of 36.4mm. This is the distance between the nut on the guitar and the first fret. It almost corresponds with the distance between the centre of the low C hole, if you have a low B flute, and the low C♯ hole on your flute.

The next section will take you further into the calculation of flute scales and the various factors which govern the alterations to them. It is here for those players who are curious about this subject and wish to know more. For most players who have an aversion to facts and figures, this next section overleaf can be safely skipped! You can read a plain language summary of this section beginning on page 171.

THE CALCULATION OF FLUTE SCALES

Firstly, we will look at some history on which this section is based.

The modern scale work started with Albert Cooper, the London flute maker who formerly worked for Rudall, Carte & Co. in the 1950s. While there, he became interested in the different scales of the flutes he received for repair. Many were made to be played at either A = 435Hz or A = 437Hz. In the 1950s and 60s, performers were playing these at A = 440Hz or higher, and were complaining about the pitch.

When Cooper left Rudall & Carte to set up on his own as a maker, he devised a scale which he used for about 10 flutes based on what he saw as the 'faults and virtues' of the scales he had measured at R&C. As he said in later years:

> *'I then abandoned this for a mathematically-calculated scale which I altered a little as the years went by, mostly according to certain criticisms levelled at it.'*

After he left Rudall & Carte, he met Elmer Cole, a London principal, who was also interested in the modernising of flute scales. He had already recalculated the tone hole positions according to Boehm's Schema of 1847, but found that there were more adjustments to be made for it to be playable at higher pitches demanded by modern times. During this period, William Bennett, also dissatisfied with his flute scale, frequently moved the tone holes on his flute according to his aural and performing experience. Richard Lee, another London player, was similarly interested in retuning his flute and experimenting. During this flute scale activity, the three often spoke to Albert Cooper whose home became a 'clearing house' where they met and discussed their various findings. There were British orchestral players who were also interested in these goings-on, some well-known soloists too, who ordered flutes from Cooper.

At this point, it is important to appreciate that once a basic scale has been calculated, there are 'corrections' or alterations to be made to the position of the tone holes before making a flute:

- The *octave length* has been calculated for a flute with a tone hole diameter of 16mm, the largest size, after which the pitch is hardly affected. For practical purposes, the tone holes need to be graduated, that is, they must progressively get smaller as the scale ascends.

This is for tonal reasons. There are more than a dozen tone holes, and although it is possible to have progressively smaller sizes as the scale ascends, more than 14 different hole sizes, for manufacturing reasons, is impractical. To graduate the tone holes in this way would require many extra and unnecessary tools. A compromise is to have around five different groups of sizes with each group becoming smaller, as the scale ascends. A smaller tone hole will need moving to a sharper position because smaller holes flatten a note. An example is the thumb hole, C_2, which is smaller than 16mm, as you can see by looking at your own flute. It is typically between 12.5 and 13.5mm in diameter. As this has been reduced, it needs sharpening (moving north, nearer the head joint) by around 3.5mm, or it would play flat.

- The five open hole notes of a 'French style' flute (E, F, F♯, A and A♯) should be moved down (south), thereby flattening them by about 1.5mm to compensate for the sharpening effect of the open cups.

- Some third-octave notes are sharp, and ideas to help these without affecting the intonation of the first two octaves have been suggested. A smaller C_2 thumb hole placed higher up the tube, or half-closing the thumb key will help make a better tone for G_3. Similarly, a smaller G♯ hole placed higher up the tube will help the tone of G♯$_3$.

- A final consideration is the key cup height above the tone holes. Some makers like to keep the key height lower because the flute will 'feel smoother' when the player plays quickly. The key cups above the holes have a flattening effect, more so the lower they are. The scales calculated here will work well if a reasonable height for the keys above the tone holes is established. As a guide, the foot keys should be 4.5mm above holes measured at the front of the key cup, the widest opening. The right-hand key cups should be at 4mm and the left-hand key cups at 3.5mm. If the keys cups are below these figures, the notes will be flatter and less resonant — the performer may feel that the flute is 'stuffy'. The air vibrates above the tone hole in a curved cone shape. The peak of the cone is about 6/10ths of the diameter of the tone hole above it. So you can see that if a key cup and pad are set below this height, it will have a flattening effect. That said, the keys cannot be too far above the holes, or the mechanism would feel clumsy.

Let us look at each of the points above. The *octave length* has been dealt with already, though there are still other opinions about this. William Bennett, Eldred Spell and the author are all of the opinion that this should be 324.1mm, which is fine for performing at between A = 440 and 441. The *octave length* was arrived at by trying flutes made with other scale lengths and experimentally altering many flutes, all while playing them professionally over many years.

Some flute makers have different octave lengths presumably because of different embouchures. At one time, for A = 440, a longer octave length of 327mm (12.874") was thought to be correct and also a shorter one of 323mm (12.716") was also used by some makers.

Albert Cooper soon realised from London performers' criticisms that Boehm's Schema produced a scale in which the left-hand tone holes were too close together, making them sharp, and the right-hand tone holes were too far apart, producing flat low notes. His solution was to split the scale in two using a sharper version for the right hand and the usual one for the left. Elmer Cole worked on a different scale to try to correct these problems — both were variants of the same idea. Cooper also later sharpened the top three notes; A♯, B, C, and C♯.

For a 440 flute, Cooper was using an octave length from C_1 to C_2 of 325mm and for a 442 flute, a shorter scale at 322.6mm. Later still, after some years of playing Cooper Scale flutes, it was suggested to him that the 442 scale was really best for performing at 440. In fact, Cooper shortened all the higher scales, 442 and 444, accordingly. As the scale developed and the professional players gave him feedback, Cooper updated the figures and gave the latest ones to those flute makers who asked for them. Eventually, he worked with US flute makers, the Brannen Brothers who still make Cooper scale flutes today.

Back to the scale calculation: using an octave length of 324.1mm and therefore a scale length of 648.2mm; divide this by 17.834 to give the position of the C♯ tone hole, measured from the centre of the C hole. To find the next hole, D (or the second fret on a guitar), subtract the C♯ tone hole measurement of 36.3mm from the original *sounding (scale) length* (648.2mm). The same process is then repeated: this sum is divided by 17.834 which will give the position of the D tone hole, 34.31mm. (611.9 divided by 17.834 equals 34.31.)

In flute making or engineering, it is always better to measure from one fixed point, or we would be measuring each tone hole from the one before, which could easily generate mistakes. We will measure all the tone holes from the centre of C_1 tone hole as a fixed point.

If the position for D (34.31mm) is added to that of C♯ (36.35), it equals 70.66mm, the distance from C_1 to D_1.

To find E♭, subtract the position for D (70.66) from the sounding length to give 577.54. Divide that sum by 17.834 and you will have the distance from C♯ to D, 32.38mm. Now, add that to the D tone hole position (70.66) to give the distance from C_1 to E♭$_1$, 103.04mm.

This process is repeated until all 12 semitones have been calculated. So far, this is easy, though as set out above there are several other factors which will change the size and position of the holes.

If a few minutes is spent looking at the figure below, the process so far should be easy to understand.

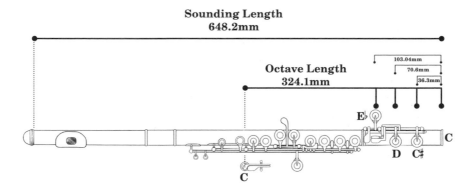

Sounding Length
648.2mm

103.04mm

70.6mm

36.3mm

Octave Length
324.1mm

E♭

C

D C♯

C

Fig. 5.5

Take a look at your own flute and you will see that the distance reduces between the first three foot joint tone holes the higher up the scale they go. Tone holes smaller than 16mm need to be moved to a sharper (northerly) position. As makers use broadly five sizes, there are slight differences between them, and so a formula needs to be established to decide how far 'north' the smaller tone holes should be moved.

Elmer Cole calculated a 'correction graph' so that any diameter of tone hole could be correctly placed.

On most flutes, the three foot holes are about 15.6mm, the four right-hand holes are 14.2mm, the left-hand are 13.5mm and the thumb C_2 and the G♯ holes often at 12.5mm with the C♯$_2$ and the two trills at 7mm. Cole's correction graph works well until we arrive at C♯$_2$, a hole which has seven uses (see Section 5.1, *Flattening a sharp C♯*).

This tone hole has been the subject of a lot of work, especially by William Bennett who is looking to find a way of playing this note with the same resonance as the rest of the octave. C♯ is a much smaller hole as you can see by looking at your flute. It is also a lot higher up than it would be compared to the thumb C_2 tone hole. The flute maker needs a correction graph to show where different sized holes should be correctly placed to play in tune.

The influence by players can be seen on some flutes where they have experienced problems with a third octave note and suggested to the maker to alter a tone hole position to correct this. Just a moment's thought by any sensible person and they will realise that the third octave is primarily the result of the tone hole positions of the first two octaves. The fingerings of the third octave differ from the first octave by opening an extra hole or two. These notes can be modified by the player using special fingerings. The third octave is sure to have intonation problems as they are founded on the third, fourth and fifth harmonics, which, as we have already seen, are not 'equally tempered'. To alter the tone holes of the first two octaves to help the third octave is the same as agreeing to spoil the intonation of two notes to help a third note!

To help you understand this better, take up your flute and finger E♭$_1$, then change to E♭$_3$ — the difference between the two is one finger, the left-hand little finger, or one extra hole open.

In the same way, compare E$_1$ to E$_3$. If there is no split-E mechanism, you take one finger off, the left-hand third finger, but there are two holes open. The extra hole makes this note harder to play. A split-E mechanism allows you to lift the left-hand third finger while only opening one hole, making that note easier to play.

Repeat with F1 and F3: it has one hole open compared to F1, not a difficult note.

F#3 has a two hole difference compared with F#1. Again, this note is harder, as we all know. To make F#3 easier will require a special Split-F# Mechanism, a costly and complicated addition which closes the A# hole while still allowing the B tone hole to open.

The third octave needs extra embouchure help and alternative fingerings. We cannot move the tone holes to 'improve' these upper notes or this will spoil the two lower octaves.

William Bennett has been experimenting for many years, altering and modifying his own flutes in an effort to get a perfect flute scale. Bennett's scale, now termed Revised Scale 2012 (RS 2012), is set out at www.trevorwye.com. This is set out for the few who may be interested in flute making. The scale is similar to Coopers but with some minor personal alterations.

It must be mentioned that Albert Cooper was the most open-minded of flutemakers, always seeking the opinions of players about scales and other improvements. In his final years, he remarked to the author:

> *'Cooper's Scale? What's that? It has been*
> *changing ever since we first began to use it!'*

He was never of the opinion that his scale was set in stone, though as far as he was concerned towards the end of his life, he had done his best and produced a perfectly workable scale. It was up to others to tinker with it if they wished.

SUMMARY

The section above sets out how the positions of the tone holes on your flute are arrived at. Here is a summary in a nutshell:

- The octave length and the scale length have to be established.

- The scale length is divided up to give the tone hole positions, with a diameter of 16mm. If flutes were actually made like this, the tone would be poor. The holes need to get smaller the further up the flute, towards the head joint that they go.

- Having holes in the key cups, such as on open hole flutes, sharpens the note. Therefore, the five open cup tone holes should be placed slightly lower, towards the foot joint.

- There are some other corrections which players have made, particularly to the left-hand notes, not based on maths but on performing experience over many years. These are already incorporated in the 'Revised Scale 2012'.

Finally, the maths has been done, and millions of flutes have been made, yet there are still intonation problems and you might well ask why.

Let's take a snapshot: A distinguished player Joe Bloggs, has been playing a certain brand for several years. If it were tested using the tests set out below, it would reveal a flat B♭ though Bloggs is used to this. A flutemaker asks Bloggs to try out a new model of flute and on testing it, Bloggs suggests that, though the their flute is a very nicely made, it has a sharp B♭. The maker agrees to flatten the B♭ knowing Bloggs to be an influential expert.

There is the problem.

To continue, as already mentioned, some makers do not flatten the five open hole notes as it makes the flute easier to manufacture. They do this to make construction easier because the bodies and key work of closed and open holed flutes are made in the same way. They assume that most players probably won't notice the difference! Actually, in the earlier stages of a performer's career, this may be true as they might not have developed good enough aural skills to detect the difference. Later, in an orchestra or when performing a solo passage *pianissimo*, they might experience problems with some notes, but assume it is something that they need to fix in their own playing. The fault, however, may lie with the maker because they did not correctly place the tone holes on the tube when it was made. More commonly, an *open hole flute* made to a *closed hole* scale means that the notes under the open hole cups E, F, F♯, A, and A♯, are a little too flat in both octaves. We need to look more closely at a particular flute before buying it, don't we?

The note names above may not be the ones which you use, but look carefully at the diagram at the beginning of the book to understand how I name the tone holes throughout this book.

Finally, the very end of the flute tube, the foot joint, is considerably wider than any tone hole at 19mm (0.748") and has a sharpening effect on the pitch as it meets the open air. All wind instruments experience this effect, so extra length is added to the end, known as an *end correction*. For a C foot at A = 440Hz, the end correction is an extra 7mm (0.275"). This means that the end of a C foot flute is (or should be) 36.3mm + 7mm, equalling 43.3mm (1.704") from the centre of the C♯ hole.

The observations above may have bewildered you, but don't worry. Even if you have only got the general idea, that is a big step forward!

All the foregoing was to establish what effect these facts and figures will have on your playing and your flute. Read on — there is more information which may help you.

CHECK THE TUNING OF YOUR FLUTE

You will need a reliable electronic tuner, preferably one with a dial and moving needle as these are easier to observe than the kind which have a light as an indicator. There are very good tuners on the web and in apps too.

When working through the tests which follow, avoid *tuning* or *correcting* notes in any way so as to prove to yourself that your flute is perfectly in tune. This is understandable, especially when you have paid a great deal of money for it. *Just accept the tuning as it is shown on the tuning machine.* This is very important, otherwise much of what follows is not much use!

Tune your flute to the meter using three notes, A1, D2, and A2. We use D2 because this note is governed by the D tone hole on the foot joint, and is quite sharp on a number of flutes. This is perhaps because makers try to make the foot joint shorter in length to make the keys more accessible to the right-hand little finger.

If D_2 is indeed sharp, then *pull out the foot joint* to flatten it. You may need to pull it out quite a distance (without it falling off!) to have any noticeable effect. Tune to A_1 and A_2 to check that the octaves are in tune. If the second octave is flat, then look at my *Practice Book One* for exercises to correct this. *It is only possible to continue when all three notes are satisfactorily in tune.*

Now, for more serious work.

Play C_1, then when you have a steady, clear note, increase the airspeed, without moving your fingers, to its second harmonic, C_2.

Overblowing to the octave
Fig. 5.6

Immediately after doing this, play the 'real' C_2 and, without taking your finger off the low C key, compare the two notes. If C_1 was in tune, the 'real' C_2 should be exactly an octave higher. Don't try to adjust it with your embouchure as often it isn't quite right and will be sharp. If this is the case, pull out the head joint until both C_1 and C_2 are exactly an octave apart.

Now, do the same test with $C\sharp_1$, overblowing it to its second harmonic, then take off your fingers to play the real $C\sharp_2$ and compare the two. $C\sharp_2$ is likely to be sharp again — probably very sharp — but this is a common problem. If you were to pull the head joint out until the two $C\sharp$s were in tune, then the two $C\sharp$s would sound as a flat octave.

If you are thinking 'What shall I do?' then you are not alone. What you are doing, of course, is checking the octave length of your flute.

Repeat the testing of the two notes, $C\natural$ and $C\sharp$, a few times to note the amount of sharpness, if any. If you have a low B, perform the same check with B_1 and B_2.

After some testing, you may want to keep the two C♮s in tune, even though the two C♯s are wide. That's fine. We will look at ways of correcting the C♯s later in Section 5.1, *Flattening a sharp C♯2*.

As there are no more foot joint notes to use, C♯2 being the highest note on the left hand, we must resort to using the third harmonic as a further check for the rest of the flute's scale. The third harmonic is a twelfth above the fundamental, and as we discovered before, harmonic twelfths are not exactly in tune with equal temperament. This will not trouble us, as the difference is so small. The flute's twelfth and harmonic twelfth are quite close enough for our simple testing purposes.

To continue, play C1 again and overblow it to its second harmonic, C2, then to its third harmonic, G2. As before, check this third harmonic with the natural note, G2. To listen closely, go backwards and forwards between the two notes a few times, as the harmonic notes are sometimes 'fuzzy', making it hard to hear the tuning clearly. Be sure to try these intervals for some time until you are confident playing them all with a good tone, as this may affect the intonation.

At this point, it would be sensible to make a written list of individual notes which appear to be either in tune, sharp, or flat compared with the harmonics. This will help you decide later what, if anything, should be done to your flute.

Repeat the same procedure with C♯1 and its twelfth, G♯2. Then again with D1 and A2. Continue as shown below.

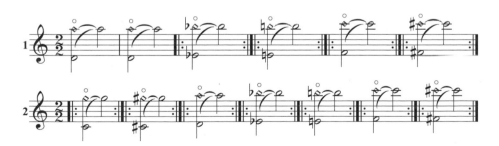

Overblowing to the third harmonic
Fig. 5.7

If you pulled out the foot joint a little to flatten D_2, make sure you push the foot back in again to check the other harmonics. You may find that the A_2 harmonic of D_1 is sharp. Repeat the checking process comparing $E\flat_1$ with $B\flat_2$, E_1 with B_2, F_1 with C_3 and, finally, $F\sharp_1$ with $C\sharp_3$. Don't be alarmed if all the notes seem to be out of tune or some notes are flat and some sharp. You should repeat this test a few more times over two or three days before deciding whether or not to do something about it. Remember to make a list to remind yourself of the sharp or flat notes.

Most commonly, the $C\sharp_2$ is very sharp, and C_2 and D_2 a little sharp, though different flutes vary. The diagram at the beginning of this book may make the naming of notes emitted from the tone holes easier to understand.

By now, after a few days of testing, you should have a list of what you suspect may be the problem notes. The next section will explain the options available to you to fix them.

HOW TO MODIFY YOUR FLUTE'S SCALE

This may be a daunting prospect to many readers who may not wish to mess about with their flutes. For them, it is better to leave well alone, but read what is to follow and, if you do fancy making some alterations, seek the advice of a repairperson to help you. Even so, reading what is to follow will still help with your understanding of flute tuning.

For those who are willing to give it a try, what follows are a few simple experiments of a non-permanent nature which will cause no harm to your flute whatsoever, if the instructions are followed carefully. After trying these, you will have the choice of continuing to the section which will involve removing key work and making small alterations to your flute's tuning. For those who are moderately experienced in maintenance and repair, this section will be worth looking at if you feel you need to improve your flute's scale.

FLATTENING A SHARP $C\sharp_2$

An easy solution to temporarily alter the pitch of any note is to use Scotch *Magic Tape* which can be stuck to the flute but, when removed, does not leave any stickiness. *Don't be tempted to use ordinary sticky tape.*

C#2 is frequently criticised for being too sharp, or of poor quality. As was described in Section 5.1, *Checking the flute scale*, the position of this note's tone hole is not standard on every flute, indicating that makers are not in agreement about its correct position. Some makers claim that this note needs to be corrected by the player, which is only partly true. Its tone does need special attention to match it with the rest of the octave, but this is far easier *when it is placed in its correct position!*

The C#2 hole, as you can see, is smaller than the other holes. It has seven functions; it plays C#2 and C#3 and it acts as a vent hole for D2, Eb2, D3, G#3 and A3. Ideally, it should be of a slightly different size to accommodate the needs of each of these notes, but as that isn't practical, the diameter of the hole is set at 7mm (0.275") which serves all seven notes — though not perfectly. Some experiments have shown that this tone hole is better with a diameter of 6.7mm (0.263"). You may think, 'Does that tiny reduction make that much difference?'. Yes. C#2 is a very sensitive note, as we all know. What works perfectly well for one note may not work as well for another. A smaller diameter hole for this note at 6.7mm has become more common on newer flutes. If this revised diameter is coupled with a taller tone hole, typically an extra one millimetre higher, then the player has a far better chance of making this note resonant, like the rest of the octave. The extra height seems to add a tiny amount of resistance which helps the player fix the tone. This means that the tone hole height — whatever it currently is — needs to be increased by an extra 1mm. It helps to make a better-quality tone and clearer octaves from C#2 to C#3, but is not something you can do yourself!

Check the pitch of both C#2 and C#3. If C#2 is sharp, place a thin strip of transparent tape across the *north* side (head joint end) of the tone hole, *sticky side down*. Be sure it is the sticky side *on top* of the tone hole and *not on the pad!* Try to cover about 1/4, or less, of the hole diameter, and then test C# using the previous experiments. Even though you have interfered with the pad seating, the flexibility of the pad should still allow it to cover the hole adequately. A few pad types are not so forgiving, in which case you won't be able to try this so successfully. You may adjust the tape covering the hole, but don't cover it too much or it will also affect the quality of the other five notes used by this hole.

C♯₂ with transparent tape
Fig. 5.8

Even with between 1/4 or a 1/5 of the tone hole covered, you may notice that the tone might be *slightly* less clear than before, but note that flattening the sharp C♯ by using the embouchure produces a *much less* clear tone! This tuning tape is a compromise, but a way of discovering what happens to the C♯ when its pitch is lowered in this way. If, after playing for a time, the result is satisfactory, your repairperson can easily remove the tape and insert a half-moon shaped piece of plastic filler in the north side of the tone hole. It should reduce the diameter of the hole by about 1/5 — the illustration below shows how it will look. Alternatively, in this next section, you can read how to do this job yourself.

HEAD JOINT ← → FOOT JOINT

Fig. 5.9

MODIFYING NOTES USING PLASTIC FILLER

You might be reluctant to remove any key work from your flute. If this bothers you, then the only way would be to take it to a repairperson to do the job for you. You can explain that you want certain notes flattened using plastic filler, or ask them to read this section. If you are doing this yourself, you will need to obtain the following tools.

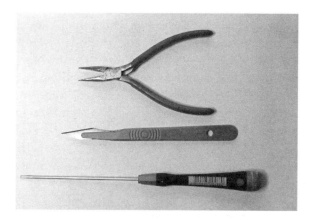

Tools
Fig. 5.10

THE TOOLS

- A screwdriver with a long blade, the end of which exactly fits the slots in the screw heads on your flute.

- A pair of small pliers, as shown above.

- You will also need some 'crocus paper', a very fine jeweller's abrasive paper for cleaning up jewellery.

- A tube of plastic filler usually found in model making shops. It dries in about 10–15 minutes.

- A small craft knife will also be useful.

The extra long screwdrivers are available from electrical suppliers such as Radio Shack, Tokyo Hands or similar electrical component stores. The length of this tool makes it far easier to extract screws and rods, especially the C♯ rod.

FLATTENING C♯2 WITH FILLER

Already, you may have tried flattening C♯2 with tape. To implement this more permanently, the tape should be substituted by placing some plastic filler in the tone hole.

On most flutes, the removal of the rod on which the C♯ key pivots is quite easy. Be sure the screwdriver head exactly fits the screw slot, and is not wider or it will scratch the pillar. While unscrewing the rod, keep a gentle pressure on the A and A♯ keys to keep them in place. When you have completely unscrewed the rod, you will hear or feel it 'click'. Then, with the pliers, remove it, and the C♯ key should be free to detach. Be aware that on some flutes this rod also holds the entire left hand mechanism — the A♯, A and G keys — in place. If this is the case, try to keep the keys roughly in place as this will make reassembly easier later.

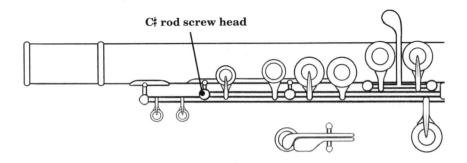

Location of the C♯ rod screw
Fig. 5.11

Before using the plastic filler, clean and slightly roughen the inside north wall of the tone hole with crocus paper, so that the filler adheres well. Don't be afraid to use this paper — it is very soft and although you won't feel much abrasiveness, it will minutely provide a secure surface for the filler to stick to. Be careful not to abrade the top lip of the tone hole upon which the pad is seated.

Squeeze out some filler onto a piece of paper, then put a small amount on your finger tip and wipe it across the top north side of the hole.

Wait until the filler is almost dry, before moulding it with the end of the screwdriver or a pencil, so that it forms a crescent shape. Make sure that the plastic crescent is smooth and a little below the top surface of the tone hole so it doesn't interfere with the pad. Use the craft knife to clean the top edge of the tone hole with the non-sharp back edge of the blade. Now, look inside the tube and make sure that no filler is hanging down as this will interfere with your usual cleaning procedure and your new C♯ correction filler may be knocked out by your cleaning stick. If there is some filler hanging down inside, while it is still pliable, use a long rod such as a wooden dowel or cleaning stick to push the moist filler back up clear of the bore. Be careful not to scratch the inside of the bore. Sometimes the filler drops out and you might have to repeat the whole operation a couple of times just to make a neat job of it, but when satisfied, leave the filler to dry and only assemble the C♯ key an hour or so later.

Do note that making the C♯ hole smaller will affect the tone of that note slightly, as mentioned before, but on the other hand, *flattening that note with your embouchure has a bigger effect on the tone*. Making the hole smaller is the better of the two options. With other, larger holes, such as the thumb C2 detailed below, the tone will hardly be affected.

FLATTENING C2 WITH FILLER

The two thumb keys will first need to be removed by unscrewing the short rod holding them in place.

Use the same procedure as for the C♯ hole above. Clean and use the crocus paper on the inside of the *north* wall of the hole. Then, place a small amount of filler in the shape of a crescent at the north end of the hole as shown in Fig. 5.12. As before, check the inside of the bore for any filler hanging down. This can be pushed up with a piece of dowel or with your cleaning stick, and removed through the tone hole.

When cleaned up and dry, replace the keys. Don't forget to check the inside of the bore. If you regularly mop out your flute, do it gently for a few days or the filler may be pushed out. Better to do it gently anyway! The C2 tone hole diameter is usually between 12mm and 13.5mm, and the aim is to reduce it by about 1–1.5mm. Some flutes may need more than this, but you will find out when playing if it needs flattening further. If so, you can remove the old filler and repeat the procedure.

A C2 tone hole with white filler placed at the 'north side'
Fig. 5.12

ALTERING THE PITCH OF OTHER SHARP NOTES

Special fingerings have already been set out in Section 2.8, *Special and sensitive fingerings*, so check there to see if a solution has already been suggested for your problem note.

The process outlined above can be repeated for any other troublesome sharp notes, though it is worth noting that the further away the holes are from the head joint, the less the flattening effect of the filler and so more will need to be used. A look at your flute will show you why: as the tube becomes longer, the tone holes are further apart. It follows that more of the filler will be required to be effective. Remember that pulling out the head joint has less effect on the pitch of the lower right-hand notes than those in the left hand.

An easier method of flattening the five tone holes under the open cups (tone holes A♯, A, F♯, F and E) is to plug the holes with small corks, or you could simply cover each hole with a small piece of transparent 'magic' tape. This has the effect of flattening these holes by about 1.3mm — not much, but it will help. There are commercial plugs available too.

If you are unfortunate to have a flute which has a very faulty scale, it may be better to replace it at some point. It will make your flute-playing life easier, and if you are a student it may help in getting work since you would be more likely to play in tune. Alternatively, you could get your flute tuned by a flute repairperson who specialises in retuning flutes, but this is a very costly operation and should only be considered on a favourite flute — one which you feel you are likely to be playing for life. This costly retuning process involves removing some tone holes, soldering them onto a piece of spare tube, cutting out the section of the tube containing the tone hole and soldering it back on the flute in a different position. My flute is one of several which have had this operation on every hole because it was originally pitched at A = 435. A photo below shows the tone holes with patches to the right of each, showing that these were flattened to the south.

Bonneville flute after retuning
Fig. 5.13

Rest assured, this tuning process does not affect the tone in any way, though the operation also requires extensive key work alteration to allow the cups and pads to cover the tone holes in their new position. After the flute has been padded and adjusted, it may appear to play better — probably the result of a more helpful scale. It is often thought to be well worth the effort as the player should now have the freedom to play expressively without having to bend some notes to play them in tune.

You may be wondering if a properly or improperly-tuned flute is apparent to the listener. In an international flute competition in 2012, I listened to 40 first-round players and, as a side detail, I decided to guess the make of flute the performer was playing, purely by the intonation. After the first-round results were announced, some players came to the jury to ask for their criticism. I helped them and also told them which flute I thought they had played. Out of the 13 players who sought advice, I was correct in naming nine of them. Some of these were obvious as there were a couple of flutes with a flat A and A♯, and a sharp C and C♯, which pointed to a particular brand which has those problems. On other flutes, when the interval B♭ to C was played, it was too large, allowing a reasonable guess as to its provenance. In some cases, it was a toss-up between two flutes which happened to have similar tuning problems in some areas. In each case, the player was surprised to know that their flute was recognisable by its intonation. It is worth remembering that after some time, perhaps after years of playing a particular instrument, *the player becomes uncritically accustomed to its defects*. These players may well think other players' intonation is wrong!

A flute can be bought with a good scale. Information about such flutes can be found by asking teachers, other students, and also talking to reliable flute shop owners. I, together with Eldred Spell and William Bennett, have developed a satisfactory scale developed over many years. You can find it on my website. The best method by far is to test the new flute's intonation yourself by using the tools provided in this book — then you can be sure.

You might be wondering if other woodwind players modify the tuning of their instruments. I remember sitting near the virtuoso oboist Neil Black in an orchestra and watching him apply 'shellac', a thick glue, to the inside north face of an oboe tone hole which he felt was too sharp.

RETUNING FLAT NOTES

Supposing you have some flat notes? Unfortunately, they can't be sharpened without major work, so you have two options. The first requires you to be aware that a particular note is flat when performing so that you can adjust it with your embouchure. The second option is, if there are several flat notes, to push the head joint in so that these notes are now in tune. Then, the remainder of the notes, which have now become too sharp, can be flattened as outlined earlier.

5.2 DEALING WITH OTHER PROBLEM NOTES

A FLAT HIGH D

This is a common problem. D3 requires a properly set up C#2 hole and a correctly positioned G hole. Even then, D3 often still seems to be a little low. (Also see Section 2.8 for special fingerings.) If the G tone hole has been placed too low, then G1 and G2 will be flat, and D3 more so. The only solution is to raise the D with the embouchure as a deliberate movement each time it is played so that it becomes habitual. If the G tone hole is also thought to be too flat as well, it can be sharpened by your repairperson by scraping out a little of the tone hole wall at the *north end* (the *head joint* end) of the hole. Check its position with the diagram at the front of this book. Only a small amount should be safely removed — your technician will know how much care needs to be taken with this operation. Otherwise, make it a habit to sharpen it when practising.

THIRD-OCTAVE TUNING

Quite often, E♭3 follows on from D3. E♭ being a sharp note, it emphasises the flatness of the D. A smart player will flatten E♭3 and sharpen D3 with the embouchure to minimise this wide interval. Similarly, E3 often follows on from D3 and the same rule applies: flatten E3 either with the embouchure or by fingering it *without* the E♭ key (right-hand little finger). Again, when F♯3 follows on from D3 as in D major, a major third, it needs an even flatter F♯3 to play expressively. You could use the middle finger — but even then it may not be enough to flatten it and you will also need to use your embouchure to bring the note back into tune.

It is interesting to note that most players play D3 flat and E♭3 sharp — check it with an electronic tuner and you may be surprised at the result. After some years of playing at these pitches, our ears become accustomed to the out-of-tuneness. For *pianissimo* notes, add the C♯1 key for both F3 and F♯3 and A3. These and other special fingerings are set out in 2.8, *Special and sensitive fingerings*.

5.3 TEST YOUR TUNING SKILLS

TEST YOURSELF

Find a simple melody to practise, such as Philippe Gaubert's 'Madrigal' on the next page. In this melody, the chords below the tune will determine the direction of any bending of pitch. On the first beat of the first bar, the chord is A minor — C2, which is the minor third, should be sharper. The B in the second bar is a major third and sounds better when flatter. In the third bar, the G2, a minor third, should be raised. The F♯ in the fourth bar (the third of D major) is better flatter, and the resolution to the phrase (low D) should be raised as it is the fifth of G major. This sort of exercise may give an insight into how small changes can make a phrase sound more expressive. Though these pitch changes are small, they add to the effectiveness of the expression.

If you think this is too fussy an approach, that's fine. To play this melody in equal temperament is perfectly satisfactory. If you play the intervals sharp when they should be flat, and vice versa, it will sound bad, for example, if the B in the second bar of the 'Madrigal' is played sharp instead of flat. Try this exercise over a few days to begin to appreciate how expressive slightly-altered intervals can sound.

Gaubert: Madrigal
Fig. 5.14

These are small changes to equal temperament, but what is important here is not whether you are playing in *just intonation* but that you are not playing *sharp* major thirds, *flat* fifths, *sharp* dominant sevenths or *flat* minor thirds. Your ear will determine just what sounds best, and when there is confusion, the interval 'rules' will set matters straight. The chart below will help make this clear.

Equal Tempered Scale

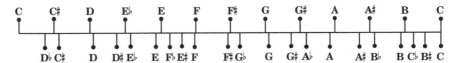

Just Scale

A comparison chart between equal and just intonation
Fig. 5.15

There are charts on pages 9 and 11 in my *Practice Book Four*: *Intonation and Vibrato* to show how to modify these and other intervals. There is also a list of pieces including some tricky orchestral works which feature intonation problems. The book also contains *24 Intonation Studies* — simple tunes to help you practise easy intervals and bend notes as necessary. You will find one study in each key and they use the most common intervals.

The 'Entr'acte' from *Carmen* (Fig. 5.16 on the next page) can be checked in this way: play low E♭ and overblow it up to its third harmonic, B♭2. Check this with the normal B♭2 in the second bar to check it isn't either flat or sharp. Top D3 is usually flat and top E♭3 is sharp as mentioned before. In the fifth bar when these two notes are next to each other, sharpen D3 a little, but reduce the *difference* between them by flattening E♭3. To check, play G2 as the third harmonic of low C. Then play E♭3 as the fourth harmonic of E♭1 or, in each case you could use an electronic tuner instead of harmonics, though it is better for your ears to distinguish correct intonation. As mentioned before, D3 and E♭3 are often at variance with equal temperament.

If you still have difficulty, you can also practise Reichert's *7 Daily Exercises*, No. 2, for the intonation of simple intervals. It contains plenty of thirds and fifths and helps you appreciate the interval intonations.

A flutist called Marion Grey
was inclined to play sharper each day.
The pitch reached a height
where the lady, one night
played the Mozart G Major in A.

TW

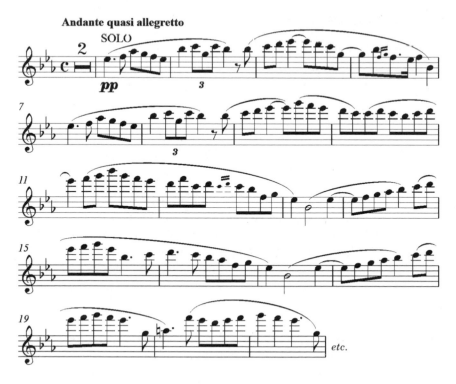

Bizet 'Entr'acte' from Carmen
Fig. 5.16

Over time, your awareness of the intonation in the key of E♭ major will be more acute. You can transfer this awareness to other keys by transposing this solo up a semitone into E major. Compare the third harmonic of low E (B_2) with the natural B_2 and then flatten both $D\#_3$ and E_3, normally sharp notes.

The next stage is to check your results with an electronic tuner to underline what you have learned in these two keys and to make sure your ears are not playing tricks on you.

Another good tune featuring easy-to-hear thirds and fifths is the Bizet melody in Fig. 5.17 on the next page. After playing through the first eight bars of the tune, play the third harmonic of E♭$_1$ (B♭$_2$) to check that you are not flat.

Provided that the pitch of the starting note G (the major third in E♭) is not sharp, then the B♭ in the fourth bar should be easier to pitch correctly. Be sure that the *pianissimo* F_2 in bar 9 and the E♭$_2$ in bar 10 are not flat.

Bizet: 'Minuet' from L'Arlesienne
Fig. 5.17

It is well worth transposing this tune a semitone down to D major to check the three notes, D_2, $F\#_2$ and A_2, as well as the A major arpeggio in bar 6.

It might also be worthwhile to play these tunes with a tonic drone. Some players find this particularly helpful.

There are many such tunes in orchestral repertoire depending on what you need. My *Orchestral Flute Practice Book, Vol. 1* contains plenty of such tunes.

SCALE COMPARISON

Fig. 5.15 illustrates the differences between 'equal temperament' and the 'just intonation' scales. Notice the differences between sharp notes and flat notes. When the sharp and flat signs were first used hundreds of years ago, flat notes were considered to be notes *lowered a little* and sharp notes *raised a little*, but in each case, *not as much as a semitone as it is today.* This diagram may help to understand the differences.

It follows on that in the key of D major, the F♯ (a major third) and the C♯ (the major third of the dominant) should be flattened. Similarly, in the key of E♭, the A♭ and B♭ are raised a little. The sharp and flat signs had a special meaning to the early instrumentalists.

You might listen to North Indian flute players playing the *bansuri* where the accompanying drone on a stringed instrument, the *sitar*, is tuned to perfect fifths. Listen to the bagpipes or musettes where the drones are also tuned to perfect fifths.

5.4 REPAIRS AND ADJUSTMENTS

FLUTE ADJUSTMENTS

If you are unsure about repairing or adjusting your flute, that is understandable — a repairperson can help you here. A competent repairperson is valuable but a *really* good repairperson is quite uncommon. Ask your teacher or a professional player for recommendations. Regardless of your decision whether to repair your own flute, it is worth getting hold of a straightforward book which gives clear maintenance instruction so that you can acquire a basic understanding of how the flute works. This knowledge will help you gain confidence when there are problems and check that you aren't just having a 'bad tone day'. You will also be able to direct the repairperson to the problem about which you are most concerned, saving his time and your bill! An excellent repair book is *The Complete Guide to the Flute: From Acoustics and Construction to Repair and Maintenance* by J. James Phelan and Mitchell D. Brody.

A QUICK CHECK-UP

Regular use of the following process will help you. It's surprising how a flute can almost stealthily go out of adjustment and cause you anxiety and frustration. Each section will take you through the steps of a checking procedure.

For most players, once a year is fine for a check-up and a clean-oil-and-adjust, but always check your flute a few weeks before an important audition or concert so as to allow enough time to get any problems fixed. You might even need extra time if your repair is the type that needs to sit for a few days and then be rechecked. Your repairperson needs to make sure that the repair hasn't altered over time as they can sometimes do. Pads, for example, may move slightly before settling in. Key work takes time to readjust after being bent slightly. This may seem strange, but metal, whether silver, gold or any other metal, has the tendency to spring back in part to its original position, which may take some days. The harder the metal, the stronger its desire to return to its original shape after bending.

Every experienced player seems to have an intuition or 'feeling' that something isn't quite right with their flute. For example, some correctly believe that a particularly weak note usually indicates that we should look for a leak or faulty pad about a minor third above that note. Read the following section to check the whole instrument.

THE HEAD JOINT AND CORK

Checking for leaks: cover the end of the tube with the palm of your hand, then cover the lip plate with your lips and blow. If there is a leak, escaping air will be heard, most likely in the area of the cork. Before removing it for tightening, it may be better to check on its position first.

After testing for a leak if there is air escaping it will be necessary to remove the cork but make sure to *always do this from the wide, south, open end of the head joint.* The cork end of the head joint is too narrow to allow it to be removed. If you are handy with tools, buy a piece of wooden dowel 3/8ths of an inch (or around 10mm) and about 12 inches (30 cm) long. Drill a small hole in the end of the dowel about 3 or 4 mm (0.30") in diameter as shown below in Fig. 5.18. After removing the crown, the mounting screw should fit well into this hole, enabling a good grip so as to push the cork assembly south, out of the tube. If the cork has been in place for some years, this may require a hard push.

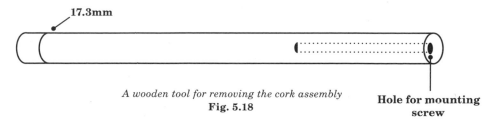

A wooden tool for removing the cork assembly
Fig. 5.18

Hole for mounting screw

Clean the cork with alcohol or methylated spirit, then add a little Vaseline and replace it to check on its tightness. If it seems too easy to place in position — or perhaps too loose — it will need to be expanded a little. To expand and compress it, clean the cork thoroughly and tighten up the small, nut-shaped end or the disc with a pair of pliers. Only a part or full turn should be required. If there is no adjustment of this kind then hold the cork six inches or more above a naked flame for a few moments. It only needs to become a little hot. *Don't burn it!* When greased and replaced, it should fit tightly.

While the cork is out, clean out the embouchure hole thoroughly with a Q-tip or cotton swab which has been dipped in rubbing alcohol. The dowel can then be used to move the cork into the correct position.

The standard cork position is calculated by using a simple formula: the diameter of the bore at the centre of the embouchure hole should be equal to the distance from the centre of that hole to the cork. This distance is usually between 17.2mm (0.677") to 17.4mm (0.685"). 17.3mm seems to be a good compromise.

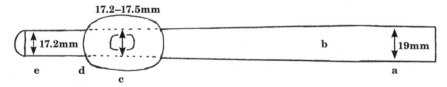

Head joint measurements
Fig. 5.19

It is a good idea to check that the line round the circumference of the end of your cleaning stick is at 17.3mm (0.681") as a few makers simply engrave a decorative line around the end so that it looks good! That said, the tone often sounds better when the cork is further out than usual, so try moving the cork an extra 0.5mm (0.019") to the *north*. This figure seems to agree with most players. Use the mark on the cleaning stick or dowel as a guide to the 'normal' position and then push the cork out a little further. You could make a second mark at 17.9mm (0.704") on the other side of the dowel. This extra distance has been recognised as the optimum placing of the cork to give both the best tone and the best third-octave intonation.

Just a final note: antique dealers are well aware that silver is a 'clean' metal. In times past, when an hygienic metal was required — such as a metal spike in meat cookery — silver was used. Its use in cutlery too is no coincidence. That's a note for those who frequently clean their head joints too!

CHECKING THE MECHANISM

Check all the keys for side-to-side movement, called 'side-play', starting with the trill keys, followed by the thumb keys, the C# key, the A# and A keys and the G key. The right-hand keys are similarly checked, followed by the foot keys. If there is *very slight* movement, it is probably nothing to be concerned about, but if there is any excessive motion it will need to be tightened. This is a simple procedure which your repairperson can do for you and will result in a more reliable mechanism. Your repairperson will have a special tool to slightly lengthen and *swage* any sleeves which have side-to-side movement and tighten them.

LEAKY PADS

To check the pads for leaks, play chromatically downwards slowly, from C#2 to low B. Note that if you are an experienced player, use a breathy *beginner's tone* as it is much easier to detect any leaks. This is because beginners typically have difficulty with the low notes, and so testing like a beginner is more likely to reveal problems. As you descend, check each key by pressing *very gently* and listening to the slight 'pop' as the note changes. If the change seems more like a tiny *glissando*, there may be a leak at that point. Remember that when you are playing quickly, the pressure on each key is much less, so your testing pressure needs only to be very light. Allow the key to rise and then gently shut it. *Repeat the notes as if you are slowly trilling, on the way down.* If you are a teacher, you may not have realised that when you check a student's flute and it seems to be working, they may still be unable to get the lowest notes. In time, you will become accustomed and more proficient in this testing technique which will help your repairperson to fix any problems. If there are any leaks, the pads will need to be readjusted by a repairperson.

As you press down, there may be a small amount of *'lost motion'* or *'double action'* on some keys, which means that it may not leak but the delay before the key closes feels a little irritating. Alternatively, when pressing a key which also closes another key, if the second key is not properly closing either the adjusting screws will need attention or some shim will be required.

FURTHER CHECKS

First, study the diagram at the front of the book to be sure you are naming the keys correctly in the text which follows.

Holding the flute horizontally, while gently holding down the A♯ key with the second finger, tap repeatedly and *gently* the B key. The A♯ key should hold down the B key when playing A. If there is movement, or lost motion of the B key, then the adjusting screw (if any) needs to be tightened by turning it about 1/16th (or less) of its circumference — the tiniest amount! If there is no adjusting screw, then you are best off consulting your repairman who will add shims to level the pad, which takes a little longer.

Now repeat this with your thumb holding down the B♭ thumb lever as if playing B♭; check the B key above by tapping it. There should be no movement. If there is movement, again, your repairperson can soon adjust it.

If you have a *Split-E Mechanism*, place your left-hand fingers on the keys as if playing G and tap the key to the right of the A key. Does that key move? It shouldn't.

Next, using any finger, hold down in turn the F♯, F and E keys whilst tapping the G key. If any movement of this key is seen, it will need to be adjusted. It should remain still.

Finally, gently hold down the low-C lever — the roller used to finger that note. Gently tap the D key. This joint is prone to getting out of adjustment due to being pushed and twisted on and off the flute a couple of times a day. You could practise assembling the foot without touching the mechanism and to twist it only in one direction. Some believe this is better for the foot joint in the long-term. The lesson here is to leave the flute out of its case in your practice room, if this is possible, and simply cover it with a cloth overnight. The flute is in three parts for ease of transport; perhaps it would be better made in one piece!

DOUBLE ACTION

This occurs when there is a 'bumpy' feeling when lowering a key that also shuts another. It simply means that the two keys are not quite in synchronisation and need adjustment. If they are out of sync, you or your repairperson will need to adjust a screw or add paper to a *clutch*, depending on which your flute has. A clutch consists of two small, free-moving plates with one pressing down on the other. If you have a clutch, a thin piece of paper can be placed between the two plates to increase pressure from one to the other. Cigarette paper is a good thin paper to use as a starting point. Alternatively, look around your house for very thin but *good quality* paper. If instead you have a screw on your flute, this may need a small adjustment by turning it about 1/10th of a turn. You will only need a very small screwdriver, no wider than the head of the screw, and one which must fit the slot as well.

OILING THE MECHANISM

If you have any doubts about your ability to do this simple task then go to see your repairperson. Better to be safe than sorry...

The finest oil for your flute is car engine oil. Fill a small bottle and there will be enough to last for many years. Car engine oil is one of the very finest, possibly due to the extremes to which it is subjected to in a fast-moving engine. The only tool needed to apply it is a needle such as one used for sewing. Do not use the end of a screwdriver as this will apply far too much. Before you begin, look at the flute's mechanism and find the spots where there are two pieces of key work revolving next to each other. The purpose of oiling is to place the *tiniest* drop in the crack between these two moving parts. The tip of the needle will hold enough oil to do this. *Only the smallest drop is needed.* This will work its way along the inside of the key and rod in time. As soon as a drop has been placed between the tubing, gently *wipe away any excess with some tissue.* This is to prevent any unused oil getting near the pads — a bad situation!

The diagram at Fig. 5.20 indicates common oiling places, however, flutes differ from each other and this is only a general guide.

Oiling as set out here is merely periodic maintenance to prevent problems arising. To oil properly means disassembling the mechanism — your repairperson will do that for you.

DAMAGE TO KEYS

Should you ever be unfortunate in damaging your flute, don't worry. This author has seen: (a) a flute savaged by a dog and the tube bitten right through; (b) two flutes which had been sat on and were banana shaped (both of which were mine!); (c) a flute with several bent keys after being dropped; and d) a solid gold head joint complete in its case which had fallen off the back of a bicycle and then run over by a bus! In each case the flute was put back to its original state, though in the case of the dog, the foot keys had to be rebuilt onto another tube. The gold head joint was squashed quite flat but Albert Cooper, a master amongst ingenious repairmen, remoulded it back into its original shape and refitted the lip plate. Curiously, this head joint seemed rather better after its accident! There is not much you can do to a flute to render it irreparable. If you have a serious accident, don't worry — it can be fixed!

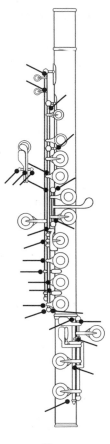

Common oiling places
Fig. 5.20

STIFF FOOT JOINT

Thoroughly clean the socket and tenon with methylated spirit or rubbing alcohol to remove all traces of tarnish or grease. Take a soft lead pencil such as a 4B and write on the tenon in small circles, all the way around, then wipe it off with a soft cloth. (It may seem strange to do this!) Repeat this, but afterwards, wiping only very lightly so you leave some remaining graphite. Insert the tenon into the socket and twist a few times to spread the graphite. This should make assembly much easier and cause less strain on the key work.

LOOSE FOOT JOINT

A loose foot joint is usually the result of careless daily assembly. Unlike a loose head joint, detailed below, if the foot joint is loose, never stick tape on the tenon as it will cause the foot to loosen even more in time. There are expensive, professional tools to tighten the foot, which your local repairperson may have access to. The foot can also be tightened by obtaining a one-foot-long piece of round wooden dowel of about half an inch in diameter. Insert most of it inside the flute body and move it in a circle, exerting a little outward pressure, on the inside of the tenon. *Do this only gently at first, checking often to see if the fit has improved.* When it has, adopt the pencil lead procedure above for a stiff foot joint to make it fit smoothly.

LOOSE HEAD JOINT

If the head joint fits too easily and loosely in the body socket, it will not respond as well as a properly fitted one. Ordinary 'magic tape' can be used temporarily for testing, but in the long term there are better solutions. Currently available is a metal (brass) tape which is highly adhesive and very thin. This can be used to make the fit tighter and it seems to last for many months. It is not cheap but will repay the outlay in time.

A loose head joint is a leaky head joint!

DUSTY MECHANISM

Rather than blowing the dust away with your breath, which may also add some spittle, scraps of food and other matter, use a pressurised air can. The can contains pure air together with a propellant, so follow the instructions carefully on the can. This suggests giving a short burst away from the flute first to get rid of the propellant before blowing away the dust within the mechanism. The can will last a long time and can be found in most DIY stores. Alternatively, a party balloon pump, also widely available, can be used to blow away any dust. Just place the flute on a table and pump away.

5.5 SOME EXPERIMENTS TO TRY

ADDING WINGS

The head joint below has had *playdough* or *plasticene* added to the sides of the embouchure hole in imitation of the *Reform Lip Plate* shown in Fig. 1.4. Adding small sausage-shaped pieces of various sizes seems to make some head joints respond well to this treatment. It's worth a try.

Take a very small piece of plasticene or playdo and roll it between your fingers to make two tiny sausages. Place where shown in the photo below and flatten them a little with your finger. They shouldn't be too long, not as far as the part of the lip plate where the air is directed. Just experiment with the position and size of the wings.

You should test the positioning to get the best result. It won't make a *huge* difference, but it is noticeable. It's not clear why this works. The two 'wings' in the illustration below are perhaps too wide: thinner ones should be tried as well.

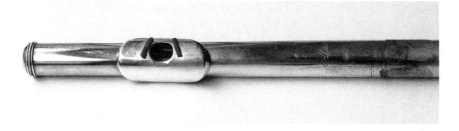

'Playdough' wings
Fig. 5.21

'WYE'S CORK', THE CORK INSERT

Take a 3/4" (19mm) cork, and cut a finger's width slice off across the diameter. Now make a hole of about the thickness of a pencil through the middle and insert into the end of your flute's foot joint. See the pictures in Fig. 5.22.

Cork insert
Fig. 5.22

After fitting it, low B or low C, depending on your flute, will not be available, however, the purpose of the cork is to enhance the harmonics of notes in the second octave. E2, for example, becomes resonant and bright. If you wish to play the middle register strongly for a short time, this might help. As a frequent performer on a B-flat flute, I use a cork insert almost all of the time, except when low C is required. It makes the right-hand notes of the second octave easier and less prone to cracking. A similar insert was tried on an alto flute, giving the same effect but less marked. More experiments using this are worth a try.

No doubt, when this book is published, some entrepreneur will claim to have invented it and will then manufacture it in 14k gold presented in a silk-lined case to be sold to the ever credulous and gullible player at a flute convention...

THE SOUND BRIDGE

This is a piece of steel which bridges the head joint tube to the socket, and is said to 'transmit' the tone, or its harmonics, to the flute body, thereby enhancing the tone. The commercial ones are two pieces of metal placed on top of each other and are widely available with varying reports of success.

I have made several kinds in four sizes. The most popular one links a single metal bridge from the head joint to the main flute body, arching over the head joint socket. The bridges can easily be cut from a thin sheet of mild steel, available at DIY stores, using metal shears. They should be bent to shape using pliers and then sanded and polished. They can be used as they are, but it is better to harden them for frequent use. To do this, heat the metal to a red colour using a blowtorch and then drop immediately into cold water. This action will 'blue' the steel, hardening it to make it springy. Some elastic tape can be attached and a couple of small patches of 'velcro' glued on to hold the device in place, as shown in Fig. 5.23. Alternatively, an elasticised hair band will also do the job. All the bridges are placed either on the front and back or side by side around the flute socket. None are placed on top of each other as in the commercial ones.

The first is two metal plates which were bought in a hardware shop as the parts which receive the lock in a door frame (these are quite solid) — they were bent and filed to shape; another bridges the head joint to its socket; the third has curved 'wings' which wrap around the flute without actually touching it; and the fourth bridges the head joint to the flute body, arching over the head joint socket. In all cases, the bridges have two tiny points underneath each end which rest on the flute head and body, and are the only parts which touch it.

Sound bridges
Fig. 5.23

These were tested over a period of a couple of weeks and almost all were received enthusiastically with different levels of opinion, but examples two and four were preferred.

They look crude but this will *not* affect the acoustics! Be sure to polish the metal areas that come into contact with the flute to avoid scratches.

Fig. 5.24 shows example four in position between the head and the flute body.

A sound bridge in position connecting the head with the body.
Fig. 5.24

CROWNS

For many years now, some flutemakers have experimented with crowns of different materials and weights. The normal crown you have fitted to the cork assembly is replaced by a different one — different by shape and size but often by weight and material too. Needless to say, the material is going to be an expensive precious metal! Some think these are effective for a variety of reasons, while others dismiss them. Like everything, why not try them? Before parting with your money, however, try adding a weight to the cork end of your head joint. I once tried a small piece of lead sheet wrapped around the cork end of my head joint. The flute played a little differently, but couldn't be described as *better*. The real difference between the two was the cost. Try all new devices and make up your own mind.

MEASURING TOOL

Fig. 5.25 shows a handy device designed by Albert Cooper, which is sold in many London flute shops. It can measure the size and depth of the embouchure hole, as well as the angle of the undercut. It is useful if you wish to compare different risers to make observations about their response.

Cooper's Measuring Tool
Fig. 5.25

BIBLIOGRAPHY

Alexander Technique

Alcantara, Pedro de. *Indirect Procedures*
(2nd edition)

Flute History and Development

Baines, Anthony. *Woodwind Instruments and their History*
(Dover)
An excellent general history book. Very informative, interesting, easy to read
and connects with the other woodwinds.

Bate, Phillip. *The Flute*
(Benn)
Very detailed, one of the most important books on the flute since 1950

Brown, Rachel. *The Early Flute*
(Cambridge, Handbooks to the Historical Performance of Music)
A very good introduction to all periods from 1700–1900

Dorgueille, Claude. *The French Flute School* (Tony Bingham)

Fitzgibbon, H.M. *The Story of the Flute*
(Reeves-London, Scribner)
Also published under 'Forgotten Books' as a paperback. Orig. published in 1914.

Solum, John. *The Early Flute*
(Oxford University Press. 1995)
A very good introduction.

Toff, Nancy. *The Development of the Modern Flute*
(Univ. of Illinois Press)
Recommended reading on flute history.

The Flute Book
(Scribner and Oxford Musical Instrument Series)
Excellent general book on all aspects of development and history.

Welch, Christopher. *History of the Boehm Flute*
(Rudall, Carte and Co., 1896 – More recent: Scholars Choice Edition)
Short and long version available. Contradicts Rockstro's version of the development of the flute.

Repertoire

Pierreuse, Bernard. *Flute Literature*
(Editions Musicales Transatlantiques [later: Jobert, Paris])
Very Useful. Also available on a CD. The book is telephone-directory size.

Vester, Franz. *Flute Repertoire Catalogue*
(Musica Rara, 1967)
Long out of print. Get it if you can; it is large paperback size. Some misprints.
There is a later selective catalogue.

Vester, Franz. *Flute Music of the Eighteenth Century*

Orchestral Repertoire

Wye and Morris. *Orchestral Practice Books 1 & 2*
Approx. 1,100 orchestral extracts. Includes the top most-popular
28 audition pieces some with orch. cues.

Wion, John. Opera Extracts for Flute. (Solum. 9 volumes.)
For those auditioning for an opera orchestra, these are a must.

General Information

Maclagan, Susan J. *A Dictionary for the Modern Flutist*
(Lanham, Maryland: Scarecrow Press, Inc. 2009. Revised and reprinted 2018)

Style

Dart, Thurston. *The Interpretation of Music*
(Hutchinson; 4 rev. edition)
Easy to read and sensible approach to early music

Mozart Concerto in G and D major
(Novello)
This editions contains helpful advice on writing cadenzas.

Technical Books

Andersen, Joachim. *24 Studies, Op. 15*
(Novello)
There are many other Andersen studies and can be found online.

Dick, Robert. *The Other Flute*
(Mel Bay Publications, Inc. Ref: DIC011)

Circular Breathing for the Flutist
(De Haske Publications)

Dehnhard, Tilmann. *The New Flute*
(With DVD. UE35320)
All contemporary techniques easily explained, including beatboxing.

Kynaston, Trent. *Circular Breathing For the Wind Performer*
(Alfred Publishing, Oct 1982)

Moyse, Marcel. *Technical Mastery for the Virtuoso Flutist*
(Zimmermann)
Now out of print but summarised in this book in Fig. 2.6.

24 Little Melodious Studies
(Leduc)

25 Little Melodious Studies
(Leduc)

Daily Exercises (480 Exercises)
(Leduc)

Soussmann, Heinrich. *24 Daily Exercises, Op. 53*
(Leduc)

Wye, Trevor. *Efficient Practice*
(Falls House Press, USA)

Wye, Trevor. *Practice Books 1–6*
(Novello rev. edition 2015)
1 Tone; 2 Technique; 3 Articulation; 4 Intonation and Vibrato;
5 Breathing and Scales; 6 Advanced Practice

Wye, Trevor, *Proper Flute Playing*
A Companion book to the Practice Book series

Wye, Trevor. *Complete Daily Exercises*
(Novello)

Piccolo

Morris, Patricia. *The Piccolo Study Book*
(Novello)

Wye, Trevor & Morris, Patricia. *The Piccolo Practice Book*
(Novello)
Complete orchestral repertoire for piccolo.

Stage Fright

Cutler, David. *The Savvy Musician*
(Helius Press)
Paperback

Greene, Don. *Fight Your Fear And Win: (7 Skills for performing your best under pressure)*
(Ed. Kindle)

Johnston, Phillip. *The Practice Spot Guide to Promoting your Teaching*
(Self published)

Jones, Kate. *Keeping Your Nerve!*
(Faber)

Ristaad, Eloise. *A Soprano Standing on Her Head*
(Real People Press, USA.)
Paperback

Tomlinson, Charlotte. *Keep Calm and Pass Your Music Exam*
(Chester Music)

Body Mapping

Pearson, Lea. *Body Mapping for Flutists*
(Pearson, 2006)

Musical Psychology

Seashore, Carl. *The Psychology of Music*
(Dover)
A great classic and easy to read.

Acoustics

Arthur H. Benade. *Horns, Strings and Harmony*
(Dover 1992)
It has helped many to understand the fundamentals of acoustics and an easy way.

Careers

Davies, Richard. *Becoming an Orchestral Musician*
A guide for aspiring professionals.

General Information

Floyd, Angeleita. *The Gilbert Legacy*
(Winzer Press, USA)
Excellent biography and very helpful about performing matters.

Nyfenger, Thomas. *Music and the Flute*
(Flute World Publications, USA)
One of the great teachers and players who received minimal public recognition.

Wye, Trevor. *Marcel Moyse, An Extraordinary Man: A Musical Biography*
(Winzer Press, USA)
All you wanted to know about this great flutist.

Wye, Trevor. *Fantastic Flutes*
(Spartan Press)
60 or more other things you can do with flutes!

Repair and Adjustments

Phelan, James. *The Complete Guide to the Flute and Piccolo:*
From Acoustics and Construction to Repair and Maintenance
(Conservatory Publications, USA. 2005)

Smith, J. *Servicing the Flute*
(Independent)
Very helpful and with pictures.

TREVOR WYE: PRACTICE BOOKS FOR THE FLUTE:

OMNIBUS EDITION BOOKS 1–6 (BOOK ONLY)
NOV164186

OMNIBUS EDITION BOOKS 1–6 (BOOK/CD)
NOV164967

REVISED EDITION BOOK 1: TONE (BOOK/CD)
NOV164109

REVISED EDITION BOOK 2: TECHNIQUE (BOOK ONLY)
NOV164131

REVISED EDITION BOOK 3: ARTICULATION
(BOOK ONLY)
NOV164142

REVISED EDITION BOOK 4: INTONATION & VIBRATO
(BOOK ONLY)
NOV164153

REVISED EDITION BOOK 5: BREATHING AND SCALES
(BOOK ONLY)
NOV164164

REVISED EDITION BOOK 6: ADVANCED PRACTICE
(BOOK ONLY)
NOV164175

COMPLETE DAILY EXERCISES
NOV120850

PROPER FLUTE PLAYING
NOV120651

OTHER METHOD BOOKS:

FLUTE CLASS GROUP INSTRUCTION BOOK
NOV120738

TREVOR WYE'S VERY FIRST FLUTE BOOK
NOV120783

A BEGINNERS BOOK FOR THE FLUTE: PART 1
(BOOK ONLY)
NOV120584

A BEGINNER'S BOOK FOR THE FLUTE: PART 1
(BOOK/CD)
NOV120848

A BEGINNERS BOOK FOR THE FLUTE: PART 2
(BOOK ONLY)
NOV120585

A BEGINNERS BOOK FOR THE FLUTE: PART 2
(BOOK/CD)
NOV120849

**A BEGINNERS BOOK FOR THE FLUTE: PARTS 1 & 2 –
PIANO ACCOMPANIMENT**
NOV120586

**TREVOR WYE/PATRICIA MORRIS:
THE ORCHESTRAL FLUTE PRACTICE: BOOK 1**
NOV120801

**TREVOR WYE/PATRICIA MORRIS:
THE ORCHESTRAL FLUTE PRACTICE: BOOK 2**
NOV120802

**TREVOR WYE/PATRICIA MORRIS:
THE ALTO FLUTE PRACTICE BOOK**
NOV120781

**TREVOR WYE/PATRICIA MORRIS:
PRACTICE BOOK FOR THE PICCOLO**
NOV120658

TREVOR WYE COMPILATIONS:

A VERY EASY FLUTE TREASURY
NOV120852

A VERY EASY 20TH-CENTURY ALBUM
NOV120682

A FIRST LATIN-AMERICAN FLUTE ALBUM
NOV120634

A SECOND LATIN-AMERICAN FLUTE ALBUM
NOV120635

FOR FLUTE ENSEMBLES:

**TREVOR WYE:
FLUTE CLASS CONCERT ALBUM
FOR FLUTE ENSEMBLES**
NOV120784

**TREVOR WYE: THREE BRILLIANT SHOWPIECES
FOR FLUTE ENSEMBLE (SCORE)**
NOV120685

**TREVOR WYE: THREE BRILLIANT SHOWPIECES
FOR FLUTE ENSEMBLE (PARTS)**
NOV120685-01